POSITIVE BEHAVIOUR STRATEGIES TO SUPPORT CHILDREN AND YOUNG PEOPLE WITH AUTISM

D0882202

POSITIVE BEHAVIOUR STRATEGIES TO SUPPORT CHILDREN AND YOUNG PEOPLE WITH AUTISM

Martin Hanbury

LIBRARY
FRANKLIN PIERCE UNIVERSITY
RINDGE, NH 03461

Paul Chapman
Publishing

© Martin Hanbury 2007

First published 2007

Apart from any fair dealing for the purposes of research or
private study, or criticism or review, as permitted under the
Copyright, Designs and Patents Act, 1988, this publication
may be reproduced, stored or transmitted in any form, or by
any means, only with the prior permission in writing of the
publishers, or in the case of reprographic reproduction, in
accordance with the terms of licences issued by the Copyright
Licensing Agency. Enquiries concerning reproduction outside
those terms should be sent to the publishers.

SAGE Publications Ltd
1 Oliver's Yard
55 City Road
London EC1Y 1SP

SAGE Publications Inc.
2455 Teller Road
Thousand Oaks, California 91320

SAGE Publications India Pvt Ltd
B 1/I 1 Mohan Cooperative Industrial Area
Mathura Road, Post Bag 7
New Delhi 110 044
India

SAGE Publications Asia-Pacific Pte Ltd
33 Pekin Street #02-01
Far East Square
Singapore 048763

Library of Congress Control Number: 2007924947

British Library Cataloguing in Publication Data

A catalogue record for this book is available from the British Library

ISBN 978-1-4129-2910-3
ISBN 978-1-4129-2911-0 (pbk)

Typeset by C&M Digitals (P) Ltd, Chennai, India
Printed in Great Britain by the Cromwell Press, Trowbridge, Wiltshire
Printed on paper from sustainable resources

This book is dedicated to
Theresa O'Donovan

CONTENTS

ABOUT THE AUTHOR

Martin Hanbury is headteacher of Landgate School, Bryn a specialist school for pupils with autism in North-West England. Martin has worked with people with autism for over twenty years in a variety of roles including carer, play worker, teaching assistant, teacher and school manager. He is currently collaborating with a range of agencies in the development of services for people with autism in his locality and serves on the National Autistic Society's Accreditation Programme as a team member, team leader and panel member.

Martin holds Masters' degrees in Special Education, Educational Management and Research Methodology and a PhD focusing on Educational Leadership. He works as a Regional Tutor on the University of Birmingham's Webautism Programme and is Associate Tutor with the University of Edge Hill, contributing to their Professional Development Programmes focusing on Autistic Spectrum Disorders.

Having published *Educating Pupils with Autistic Spectrum Disorders: A Practical Guide* in 2005, Martin provides training programmes focusing on a range of issues related to Autistic Spectrum Disorders, particularly in the area of challenging behaviour.

FOREWORD

Over the last decade the number of books available to support the understanding of individuals on the autistic spectrum has soared. For parents, family and practitioners to develop their understanding, it is essential that the investment of time in reading results in practical advice that influences practice. This book fills this need.

Having worked with the author for a number of years and experienced first hand his work with children and young people across the autistic spectrum, I can recommend the theory and the strategies included in this book as tried and tested. The case studies sprinkled into the body of the text provide a clear focus on the need to address individual needs with a person-centred approach. Martin's commitment to improving the lives of individuals on the autistic spectrum by supporting the whole person, the family and carers as well as the professionals supporting the child is evident in the chapters of this book.

The author helps the reader to understand the world as seen through the eyes of the child with autism, pointing out the complexity of the condition where there are no quick fixes to apply. It is through the commitment and tenacity of parents and professionals that positive steps forward can be achieved.

Chapter 1 provides the backdrop of understanding for autism and a working definition of challenging behaviour, reminding us that the behaviour has an impact on those supporting the child as well as the child him/herself. We are reminded in Chapter 2 that it is only through collaborative work that information can be shared and support provided consistently. The following chapters provide a balance of theory and practical strategies to improve the opportunities for the child. This includes an overview of the optimum learning environment and how this can be achieved.

Throughout the book useful tables, diagrams and proformas are provided for use by the practitioner. Models of each are given to broaden the understanding of their use. Each chapter ends with key points, drawing the theory and practice together in summary.

The final chapter addresses the issue of mutual support; family to family, professional to family and professional to professional. It includes an appendix that draws this point out by providing training materials and useful information for raising awareness on the issue of positive behaviour strategies for people with autism.

Accessible, easy to understand, based on sound experience, this book is a valuable part of the tool kit for all practitioners and parents supporting children and young people on the autistic spectrum.

Francine Brower
Regional Co-ordinator (North)
National Autistic Society

ACKNOWLEDGEMENTS

The field of autism is populated by a unique and special type of person. Individuals who experience the condition and the families and practitioners who support them are defined by qualities which mark them out from the crowd. We should celebrate their contribution to the richness and diversity of the communities around them and recognise the importance of the perspectives they offer.

In my years working with individuals with autism I have learnt something new every day simply because there is so much to be learnt. For this, I must thank the many individuals with autism who have allowed me to work alongside them and discover all I can about this complex condition. I must also thank the dedicated and courageous families and colleagues I have been fortunate enough to work with and who have guided me throughout my career.

Special thanks goes to the pupils, parents, staff team and Governing Body of Landgate School, Bryn, for their enthusiasm for learning and unstinting support.

Finally, I must thank Megan, Timothy, Patrick and Francis for their questions, insight and encouragement.

INTRODUCTION

There is no simple causal link between autism and challenging behaviour. However, there are situations in which the impact of autism on a person may cause them to act in a way which challenges other people. Many people with autism present no more challenging behaviour than people without the condition. However, for most people with autism, the world around them is a significantly challenging place, full of confusing rules, conflicting standards and strange, unpredictable happenings. Faced with the challenge of a frenetic and frightening world, it is not surprising that some people with autism respond with equally challenging behaviour.

There have been times in our history when society reacted to such challenges in a profoundly visceral and inhumane manner. Some people with autism alive today have been a part of this sorry history. Fortunately, in recent years, there has been significant progress in the way in which we understand both the condition of autism and the nature of challenging behaviour. This has led to improvements in the practice of professionals and the life quality of the majority of people with autism. Although far from a situation with which we can be satisfied, we have moved forward and there are an increasing number of examples of good practice which can be found.

This book has been inspired by examples of this high quality practice which can be found across all sectors in a wide range of contexts and is characterised by positive approaches focused on individuals' needs. Underpinning much of this effective practice is the development of proactive strategies to support positive behaviour in individuals with autism. For some individuals, in some contexts, these strategies are relatively straightforward and may be seen as an extension of established practice. For other individuals, practitioners need to employ a range of highly specialised approaches which are developed over a prolonged period of time. Whichever case pertains, effective practice is based on positive approaches supporting positive behaviour.

The purpose of this book is to share the good practice in behaviour support which has emerged in the field of autism over recent years. In order to achieve this, the book will:

- provide a brief overview of established theories of autism

- discuss a range of challenging behaviour and consider how this might emerge as a consequence of the impairments people with autism experience

- describe the underlying principles of behaviour support with a particular focus on understanding the function of behaviour in meeting a person's needs

- examine the ways in which practitioners might develop their skills, knowledge and understanding in order to effectively support people with autism who display challenging behaviour

- enable practitioners to critically evaluate the environment they operate in and work towards developing environments which are functional and supportive for people with autism

- support practitioners in developing effective approaches to teamwork, incorporating ideas for supporting the professional development of their colleagues, collaboration with families and inter-agency practice

- provide practical guidance on the development of strategies which address challenging behaviour and support the development of positive behaviour

- present a series of case studies based on actual experiences which illustrate the practical application of the principles of behaviour support.

It is the intention of the book that this practical approach towards supporting positive behaviour will complement existing publications and accredited schemes and programmes in the field. For practitioners to become truly effective in supporting positive behaviour, this book must become part of a process of developing knowledge, understanding and skills which extends to all areas of practice and remains continuous.

From the outset, this book proposes four fundamental cornerstones as the foundation of understanding behaviour support and autism. These are:

1 Autism is a complex condition which manifests itself in many different ways. Approaches to behaviour support must be flexible in order to address a broad spectrum of needs.

2 There is only one certainty in the field of autism and that is that there are no other certainties. There are several guiding principles which can be applied to most situations, but no absolute rules for effective practice.

3 There are no easy answers to the many complex issues which inhabit the field of autism. Be suspicious of quick-fix ideas and short-term solutions.

4 Practitioners in the field of autism must be open, honest, generous with their ideas, kind to themselves and utterly committed to the people they work with. Learning to live with frustrations and setbacks is a prerequisite skill; never giving in to these obstacles is an essential characteristic of the effective practitioner.

These four maxims underpin the remaining content of this book and serve to inform the development of effective behaviour support for people with autism. Supporting individuals with autism and challenging behaviour requires perseverance and commitment above anything else. Through these qualities the most difficult of problems can be overcome, as Albert Einstein himself said:

It's not that I'm so smart, it's just that I stay with problems longer.

CHAPTER 1

Autism and Challenging Behaviour

This chapter includes:

- a brief overview of current theoretical constructs of autism
- a definition of challenging behaviour for the purposes of the book
- a description of the impact of the condition on an individual's behaviour and the association between autism and challenging behaviour.

Autism: current theories

Autism is a lifelong condition which affects over half a million people in the UK alone. It is a complex, behaviourally defined condition which emerges as a result of some degree of neurological dysfunction which may be caused by a number of factors. Typically, people with autism experience a **triad of impairments** (Wing, 1996) which impacts on their development in the three key areas of:

1 Social Understanding

2 Social Communication

3 Imagination.

Understanding the profound effect of the triad of impairments on a person's life requires a recognition of the fundamental importance of these crucial areas in neuro-typical development. Children have an innate capacity to systematically acquire an understanding of the sophisticated and infinitely subtle norms of the social groups they live in. This understanding is both 'taught' and 'caught' and represents a constantly evolving ability to recognise their place in their world. This acquisition of **social understanding** is critical to the successful integration of an individual to the social group and is the fundamental building block of human society.

Inextricably linked with the acquisition of social understanding is the ability to communicate effectively within the social unit. This element of a child's development precedes spoken language and is essentially instinctive, characterised by eye contact, smiles and, as the child grows older, an increasing number of interactive initiatives led by the child. This **social**

communication acts as the binding material, the mortar through which our communities are constructed and through which human society becomes consolidated and enduring.

In the context of autism, the term **imagination** is best represented as the ability to exhibit **flexibility of thought**. This capacity is critical in enabling human beings to adapt to the complex and shifting environment we encounter day by day and minute by minute. Flexibility of thought is the core characteristic which allows us to solve problems, think creatively and develop new skills. It is a central feature of our ability to predict, speculate, experiment, discuss and adapt. It is, arguably, at the heart of all learning. If social understanding is the building block of our communities and social communication is the mortar which binds those blocks together, then flexibility of thought is the ability to design and redesign our communities. It is the architecture of our lives.

Given the fundamental importance of these three areas to an individual's development, impairments affecting these areas can be profoundly disabling. The impact of the triad of impairments will vary considerably across the spectrum with individual patterns of need representing a unique manifestation of 'the triad'. However, these difficulties arise from the same underlying features entailing that while individual needs may vary, a common root to these needs may be traced to the triad of impairments.

Alongside the triad of impairments, people with autism experience further difficulties in a number of different domains. The first of these has been termed **mindblindness** (Baron-Cohen, 1995) and relates to the apparently limited capacity of people with autism to appreciate that other people have mental processes which differ from their own. The ability to understand other people's mental states is described as a **theory of mind** and is evident from around the age of four onwards in most people. In fact, there is strong evidence of a developing theory of mind in younger children provided by their enthusiasm for involving parents and carers in focusing joint attention on the things that interest them.

As children develop, this ability to appreciate that other people are thinking and feeling differently from them is a crucial factor in developing affective relationships. The fabric of the social groups that human beings form is woven around the capacity to understand one another. Where that ability is limited or seriously impaired, it is likely that the individual will face significant obstacles in forming social relationships.

Another key area of difficulty people with autism encounter relates to a concept known as **central coherence** (Frith, 1989). Central coherence is the ability that most people have to locate meaning within a context – that is, the capacity to 'see the bigger picture'. This is a crucial feature in developing our understanding of the world as we learn to pull together the numerous stimuli we encounter moment by moment and form a coherent picture of the world around us. When this aspect of a person's understanding is disrupted, they are likely to encounter severe problems in focusing on the important elements of subjects or in generalising skills and knowledge to a range of differing contexts. People with autism typically experience difficulties with central coherence which might be manifest in their interest in minute detail, their difficulty in transferring skills from one situation to another or their limited ability to derive meaning from contextual clues.

A further difficulty that is acknowledged among people with autism is an interference in their **executive function** or the mechanism by which people move attention from one thing to another (Norman and Shallice, 1980). Executive function is a vital component in our ability to plan strategically, to prioritise our actions, to solve problems or to set ourselves meaningful objectives. If this critical system is not operating effectively, a person's ability to control their actions is markedly reduced as they become subject to the myriad influences and stimuli around them. People with autism may often appear to be highly distractible or profoundly fixated on a single item. Both these states can be related to impairment in the mechanism that allows most people to attain equilibrium between these opposites.

In addition to this, people with autism often experience significant difficulties in integrating **sensory information** which can lead to either hypo-sensitivity or hyper-sensitivity. This failure to integrate sensory information effectively causes many people with autism to react in extreme ways to sensory input. This may involve becoming over-excited by sensory input and displaying apparently uncontrolled behaviour when a particular sensory input is present. Alternatively, it may result in a person finding a particular sensory input aversive and reacting adversely when that stimulus is evident. This inability to effectively regulate the sensory relationship a person shares with the world is extremely debilitating and may account for many of the apparently bizarre behaviour patterns some people with autism display.

Consequently, we find that people with autism experience significant and profound difficulties in several critical areas of their lives. The extent to which these difficulties affect a person's life varies greatly. Some individuals with autism live completely independent lives, forming lasting, loving relationships, bringing up children, pursuing successful careers. Other people with autism live highly dependent lives in bespoke services which cater for their every need. Between these two extremes a rich and varied spectrum of needs can be found and a broad range of provision to meet those needs is gradually emerging.

Critically, this spectrum of need is not proportionately related to a person's cognitive ability. It is a general rule, that the greater the extent of a person's learning difficulty, the greater the like-lihood of that person being highly dependent on the support of others. However, in the field of autism general rules are of little use. There are many people with autism who are highly intelligent and highly dependent on other people because the impact of autism on their lives is profound and wide reaching. Therefore we cannot assume that the level of need experienced by a person can be determined through simple means. This is a field of infinite complexity.

Challenging behaviour: towards a working definition

The term 'challenging behaviour' is a broadly conceived term which is used to describe a wide range of behaviour patterns exhibited across many and varied settings. Essentially, the notion of 'challenging behaviour' is highly subjective and interpretations of the concept are as varied as the individuals who present them. This is because challenging behaviour is a personal construct; those behaviour patterns which challenge me may not challenge you and vice versa. As a personal construct, our individual perceptions of challenging behaviour reflect our own histories, ethics and sense of self-hood and are deeply rooted in the shared value systems and inherited structures of the communities we live in. Consequently, the concept of challenging behaviour is fluid, culturally defined and individually interpreted.

As a result of this, when considering individuals who may be labelled as 'challenging' we need to take into account the context surrounding those individuals and the range of factors which might have contributed to them acquiring this label. Similarly, we need to recognise the degree of support and intervention required by individuals who are termed challenging in overcoming the challenges they each encounter.

A further consequence of the subjective and fluid nature of the term 'challenging behaviour' is that it tends to elude attempts to fix an enduring definition. Various authors have described challenging behaviour as:

> behaviour that challenges – whether it is a challenge to our understanding, our own well-being or a child's or else to our ability to carry out our responsibilities as parents or professionals.
> (Whitaker, 2001, p. 4)

or

> behaviours which involve significant risks to people's well-being or act to reduce markedly access to community settings.
> (Emerson, 2001, p. 3)

While these definitions may differ in some respects, they each focus on common areas of concern, including the impact of challenging behaviour on:

- the health and safety of the individual exhibiting challenging behaviour
- the health and safety of other people around that individual
- the quality of life of the individual exhibiting challenging behaviour
- the quality of life of other people around that individual.

It is therefore possible to offer a definition of challenging behaviour for the purposes of this book as:

A working definition

Episodes or patterns of behaviour which present significant risk of harm or restriction to an individual and the people around them and are likely to be severely detrimental to the quality of life experienced by those individuals and the people around them.

Within this definition we might include five broad domains of behaviour – namely:

- Violence
- Self-injury
- Destruction
- Disruption
- Excessive self-stimulation.

These areas merge with one another for most individuals who exhibit challenging behaviour and different types of challenging behaviour might be manifest across one or several of these categories. This grouping of behaviour may be presented as shown in Table 1.1.

Table 1.1   Domains of Challenging Behaviour

Violence	Self-injury	Destruction	Disruption	Excessive self-stimulation
Behaviour directed at other people which is likely to cause injury	Behaviour directed at themselves which is likely to cause injury	Behaviour directed at the environment which is likely to cause damage	Behaviour which interferes with organised activities	Behaviour which is generally repetitive in nature and provides a reinforcing stimulus
• Attacking with objects	• Attacking with objects	• Arson	• Inciting others	• Eye-poking
• Biting	• Biting	• Pushing items over	• Refusing to move	• Flapping objects
• Hair-pulling	• Eye-gouging	• Ripping furnishings	• Running away	• Hand-flapping
• Head-butting	• Hair-pulling	• Smashing windows	• Screaming	• Masturbation
• Kicking	• Head-banging	• Smearing faeces	• Shouting	• Rocking
• Pinching	• Head-slapping	• Tearing resources		• Spinning
• Punching	• Knee-dropping			
• Pushing	• Pinching			
• Scratching	• Punching			
• Slapping	• Scratching			

P **Positive Behaviour Strategies to Support Children and Young People with Autism,**
Paul Chapman Publishing © Martin Hanbury, 2007

Through usage, the term 'challenging behaviour' has largely become associated with learning disability. The British Institute of Learning Disabilities consider that 20% of children and 15% of adults with learning disabilities exhibit challenging behaviour and that 50% of these people experience some form of physical intervention during their lifetime.

However, it must be emphasised that there is no inevitable, determining link between challenging behaviour and learning disability or between challenging behaviour and autism. Arguably, each human being exhibits challenging behaviour at regular episodes throughout their life in a conscious or unconscious effort to ensure their needs are met. These episodes are most frequent in early childhood during that period we affectionately call the 'terrible twos'. As we mature, most human beings learn to address their individual needs in more socially acceptable and sophisticated ways. This results in a decrease in challenging episodes so that they become restricted to periods of extreme anxiety or anger. Where circumstances affect this development problematic behaviour may not diminish; in fact, it may increase over time as it becomes increasingly effective in ensuring an individual's needs are met.

Factors which affect this maturation process may include autism but may also include an array of other influences such as mental health difficulties, social deprivation, family dysfunction and childhood trauma. Just as these latter factors cannot be considered as direct causal links to challenging behaviour, so too, experiencing an autism spectrum condition does not determine that an individual will display challenging behaviour. Equally, there are many individuals who display challenging behaviour and are clearly not autistic. Therefore it is more appropriate to express the relationship between autism and challenging behaviour as an association and it is the nature of this relationship which is explored below.

Challenging behaviour and autism: an association

In examining the relationship between autism spectrum conditions and challenging behaviour it is important to consider how the defining features of autism described in the early pages of this chapter might contribute to an individual developing patterns of behaviour which are challenging.

For example, if we explore each component of the **triad of impairments**, we find clear reasons why a person with difficulties in this area may develop responses which are largely considered to be inappropriate. A person whose **social understanding** is impaired does not have any frame of reference by which to monitor their behaviour and no awareness of the social norms that most people intuitively adhere to. A child without any difficulties in this area of development will quickly acquire an understanding of the approval which inevitably accompanies socially acceptable behaviour. The warm, positive feelings which this social approval evokes will reinforce the behaviour and therefore encourage further similar behaviour, establishing a virtuous cycle of positive behaviour and positive reinforcement. For a child who may not recognise our approval or who may not find our responses pleasurable, the drive towards and the maintenance of positive behaviour becomes more problematic. For many children with autism, socially appropriate behaviour is poorly rewarded by our social responses which are of little value to them.

Similarly, if a person has difficulties in deciphering **social communication**, the channels through which norms are transmitted, developed and maintained are severely disrupted. Social communication plays a critical role in providing an external means of orienting our behaviour. Within the first few weeks of life, most human beings across all socio-cultural groups learn to express and interpret a range of facial expressions. Babies quickly learn the power of the smile. As the child grows older, the ability to communicate socially becomes increasingly sophisticated so that by adulthood most people are able to interpret a vast array of subtle, nuanced signals. These signals incorporate body language, spoken words, tone of voice and an awareness of the context within which communicative acts take place.

Where this sophisticated set of skills has not developed fully, individuals may be severely disabled. Impairment in the area of social communication affects an individual's ability to:

■ address other people according to that person's expectations

■ initiate and maintain positive interactions

■ respond appropriately to facial expression

■ recognise irony, sarcasm and humour

■ discern between truth and lies

■ interpret social situations effectively.

Impaired **flexibility of thought** creates further problems. People experiencing difficulty in adapting to new situations will feel

■ powerless

■ vulnerable

■ uncomfortable

when faced with unfamiliar environments, people or activities. Therefore they are likely to limit the range of experiences they engage with in order to maintain a feeling of safety and security. Moving beyond this comfort zone may cause an individual to become anxious or frightened and provoke challenging behaviour both as a defensive mechanism and as a means of communicating fear and anxiety.

These difficulties are compounded by other features associated with autism spectrum conditions such as **mindblindness**, a limited capacity for **central coherence**, impairment in **executive function** and characteristic difficulties in effective **sensory integration**.

If a person is unable to appreciate other people's mental states, then their capacity for empathising with others may be limited. Children who are developing a fully functioning **theory of mind** might be asked to consider the feelings of other people. This empathetic referencing may not be possible for individuals with autism, thus removing a range of processes which help children to develop socially appropriate behaviour patterns.

Equally, if a person lacks the ability to **centrally cohere** a range of eclectic information into a comprehensive and comprehensible whole, they may well be unable to appreciate the impact of their actions as part of the bigger picture. Consequently, the individual may appear to act in an impulsive and illogical manner due to their limited capacity for cohering their actions into the social whole. The notion of 'sanctioning' as a consequence therefore becomes ineffective, removing yet another possible tier of intervention.

In addition to this set of difficulties, impairments in a person's **executive function** can lead to confusion and an internal chaos which is at best perplexing and at worst utterly terrifying. The inability to strategically plan your way from one situation to another might be likened to trying to find your way out of a smoke-filled room. In this frightened and confused state, many individuals may act in bizarre or aggressive ways, a response which is biologically driven and the consequence of millions of years of evolution.

Finally, the difficulties many people with autism experience in assimilating and integrating **sensory** data will further exacerbate the immense challenge of day-to-day living. Finding particular stimuli hugely aversive or intoxicatingly attractive will inevitably provoke behavioural responses which are 'off the chart'.

Similarly, whereas people with neuro-typical development are generally able to filter out non-salient stimuli in order to focus on particular matters, many people with autism are not able to do this. Therefore, while a person without autism might be able to ignore the noises from the road outside the building they are in and engage in conversation with others or effectively focus on their work, a person with autism would find every sound equally significant whether it be human dialogue or engines running.

This restricted capacity to 'filter out' sensory stimuli entails that many people with autism are often extremely fatigued, worn out by the continuous battling for attention between their senses. The state of exhaustion which many individuals with autism may experience does not result in a restful cycle of recuperation and restoration but rather significantly reduced capacities for tolerance, prolonged episodes of distress and severely compromised health.

Key points

- Autism is a behaviourally defined lifelong neurological condition which is currently conceived of across a broad spectrum of needs and strengths.

- While a single cause for autism has not been identified, there are established and credible theories which identify specific areas of impairment or difficulty as contributing to our understanding of the condition.

- Challenging behaviour is a personally constructed notion which varies significantly from individual to individual.

- Challenging behaviour is defined within socio-cultural contexts.

- Challenging, problematic or difficult behaviour is not the preserve of people with learning difficulties and/or autism. At some stage in our lives, each of us will display challenging behaviour in order to ensure our needs are met.

- There is not a deterministic link between autism and challenging behaviour.

- Challenging behaviour is driven by an individual's needs. The difficulties people with autism experience in addressing their own needs may account for any challenging behaviour they present.

Understanding Behaviour Support

This chapter includes:

■ an exploration of behaviour support including the fundamental principles underpinning this concept
■ an examination of how needs drive behaviour
■ a discussion of different types of need.

Behaviour support

Throughout this book we will focus on the notion of **behaviour support**. This is a way of thinking that has emerged among practitioners in the field of challenging behaviour since the Mid-1990s and represents a change in emphasis from more traditional approaches focused on **behaviour management**.

The key to the differences between the two concepts is contained within the terminology. Behaviour management is suggestive of one person controlling another person's behaviour through a series of externally imposed factors. Behaviour support, on the other hand, connotes an emphasis on enabling individuals to develop behaviour patterns which are productive and fulfilling for that individual. Whereas behaviour management considers how the challenges an individual presents might be modulated towards acceptability by the actions of others, behaviour support focuses on developing an individual's capacity to respond to the challenges they face in positive and valued ways. Behaviour management looks to contain a person's behaviour while behaviour support endeavours to enhance a person's repertoire of behaviour choices through proactive strategies.

Critically, behaviour support does not look on challenging behaviour as a problem that exists within an individual. Behaviour support recognises that all human behaviour occurs within a context and cannot be disassociated from contextual factors. The leading proponents in this field, LaVigna and Donnellan, comment that 'Human behaviour never occurs in a vacuum' (1986, p.18) and propose that human behaviour is a **function** of the context within which it occurs. Consequently, when considering human behaviour we must contextualise it and understand

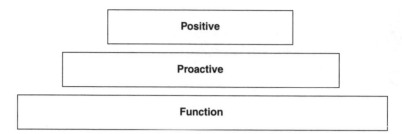

Figure 2.1   The Behaviour Support Pyramid

that it exists within a dynamic interplay of environment, interpersonal relationships and human needs. This understanding is arrived at through **functional analysis** – a process which is at the heart of all effective behaviour support.

The notion of behaviour support is constructed around three key principles which are critical in our understanding of the term – namely:

1   Behaviour is driven by an individual's needs

2   Proactive strategies support positive approaches

3   Positive approaches support positive behaviour

These three maxims build upon each other to form a pyramid with each tier of the pyramid supporting our understanding of the next level. This concept is represented in Figure 2.1 as the behaviour support pyramid.

The foundation of this conceptual model is the view that all behaviour has a function – that is, it is driven by needs and represents a means of getting those needs met. Sharing this understanding of behaviour is prerequisite to understanding support.

Having established this level of understanding as the foundation of the pyramid, it is possible to develop an awareness of the necessity to actively seek strategies which address the needs of the individual.

Through understanding this need to be proactive, there is a natural progression to understanding the need for positive approaches. In reaching this level of awareness, it is possible to develop a holistic understanding of behaviour support which builds from a sound theoretical basis towards practical, supportive intervention.

Understanding behaviour as needs driven

It is hard to imagine any human activity which does not have a purpose. Sometimes that purpose is obvious; sometimes less so. But the unifying feature of the greater part of human behaviour is that it is performing a necessary function of some sort for some reason. Behaviour occurs in order to address a person's needs and, if effective in meeting those needs, becomes an established part of their repertoire of skills.

Over time, behaviour patterns evolve in relation to the developing individual and the changing contexts in which they operate. A new-born baby's instinctive crying to communicate a need arising from hunger will invariably engage an adult carer in meeting that need. As the infant grows older, the crying gradually develops into a repertoire of language skills through which the child can request and negotiate food or drink. As the child reaches independence in this area, the use of language will become modulated into activity which enables the child to obtain their own food or drink. Consequently, within the first decade of a child's development, behaviour progresses from instinctive, reflexive responses through intentional language and towards independent actions. Yet throughout this progression, the core need, namely hunger, remains the same.

However, if a person's development is in some way impaired, there may be a limitation to the range of behaviour patterns that person acquires. Consequently, an individual with a disability may have a restricted number of behaviour options and therefore fix onto a behaviour type which has proved to be effective in addressing their needs. Therefore, considering the example referred to above, an individual whose development has been impaired may adhere to the early crying behaviour in order to address their need for food as this behaviour has worked repeatedly for them.

For most behaviour that is displayed by humans the purpose of the behaviour is easily explained. For example, I might stand in a line of people for some time moving slowly forward with each passing minute. This is because I am hungry and I am queuing up for a fast food meal. Alternatively, I may repeatedly stamp my foot on the ground. This is because I have pins and needles. Taken in isolation, either of these behaviours may seem a little bizarre; it is the context that provides meaning and the meaning which reveals the function of the behaviour.

However, there are certain patterns of human behaviour which lie further beyond straightforward explanation and appear to serve little or no logical purpose. I might bite the tip of my finger as I nervously wait for the results of an examination to arrive in the post. I may talk incessantly to a virtual stranger I have met on a train, revealing my most private thoughts and feelings. In either of these examples, the route to meaning is convoluted and therefore the function of the behaviour more difficult to interpret. Yet in both cases, the behaviour has a distinct purpose. In the first case my anxiety is to some extent controlled by the sensation of finger-biting which serves to distract me from the source of my anxiety. In the second instance, the anonymity of the fellow passenger enables me to unload a number of tensions and frustrations that have built up without any fear of judgement or prejudice. Consequently, both examples represent needs-driven behaviour which, although the needs are not directly identifiable, remains powerfully purposeful.

This aspect of human behaviour can be linked to those groups of behaviour which are identified as challenging behaviour. At a superficial level, many challenging behaviour patterns appear to serve no logical purpose. However, analysis of these behaviours reveals that basic human needs are being addressed through this pattern of behaviour.

Categories of need

These needs can be grouped into four broad categories which describe the nature of the underlying need producing the behaviour which is displayed. These needs can be understood as being related to issues which are focused around the following four areas of human need:

1 Attention

2 Tangible

3 Escape

4 Sensory.

These four areas can be further explained through more detailed definitions.

Attention: As a general rule human beings need attention. In infancy the ability to gain attention is critical in the fight for survival. As we grow older, the loving attention of other people is highly rewarding and we learn ways to focus attention on ourselves with increasingly subtle sophistication. While we might dislike individual who seem to demand our attention at all times and condemn certain people as 'attention seekers', there is within each of us an evolutionary imperative to gain the attention of those around us.

Tangible: A tangible need might be defined as any need which is directly related to an object, item or activity which an individual needs or desires. An example of this might be food or drink, a favourite toy or a matter of personal care. Every day, each of us will require the fulfilment of a myriad of tangible needs starting with drinking our first cup of coffee to wake us up, buying a newspaper to keep us in touch with the world, eating lunch to sustain us, returning to the shelter of our homes until we finally climb into bed to rest our bodies.

Escape: Escaping from dangerous or unpleasant situations is among our most basic survival mechanisms. While there might be occasions in our lives when this 'flight' instinct is triggered in real life and death situations, for the majority of us for most of the time, a moderated version of this instinct is in operation. Most commonly, this is shown as avoidance tactics – whether that be avoiding certain people, certain activities or certain demands.

Sensory: Human beings have a broad array of sensory needs which reveal themselves in a number of ways. Human beings will eat even when they are not compelled to do so by hunger simply for the pleasure of tasting particular foods. Most human beings derive great pleasure from music while many people convert that musical pleasure into dance. The sensorily located drive to procreate is perhaps the most powerful urge human beings experience and this urge in itself is a complex amalgam of sensations and responses in which virtually all of our senses are engaged.

This categorisation of need is intended to enable us to identify the root causes of behaviour which is challenging and recognise relationships between certain behaviour patterns. It is important to avoid a rigid interpretation of these categories as invariably a given behaviour may span across several categories or may emanate from one source of need and culminate in another. This is because behaviour is complex and often indeterminate. However, this four-category model can provide certain insights which support our efforts to proactively address the needs which drive behaviour. Table 2.1 is intended to illustrate this, providing a brief description of each need, a possible **communicative intent** in the behaviour and a number of behaviour patterns which may relate to the need.

Identifying needs

Frequently, a given behaviour may address several areas of need. For example, a person with autism may display self-injurious head-slapping behaviour because:

Table 2.1   Four Categories of Need

Need	Attention	Tangible	Escape	Sensory
Characteristic	Relates to an instinctive need for interaction	Relates to a specified and particular item or activity	Relates to self-preservation	Relates to deeply embedded sensations
Communication	I need you	I need this	I need to get away	I need to feel this way§
Possible	• Repetitive questioning	• Grabbing at other people's food	• Running away	• Rocking
behaviour	• Attacking others	• Stealing another person's possessions	• Isolating self from others	• Humming
patterns	• Self-injurious behaviour	• Distress due to unmet personal care needs	• Refusing eye contact	• Placing fingers in ears
	• Screaming, shouting		• Talking incessantly about a single subject	• Sniffing objects
	• Disruption		• Total passivity	• Mouthing objects
	• Destructive behaviour	• Hoarding objects	• Ignoring others	• Self-injurious behaviour
	• Excessively affectionate behaviour	• Poor personal care	• Blocking tactics	• Finger-flicking
				• Hand-flapping

(a) This immediately brings other people to them.

(b) They have a headache and are trying to relieve the pain.

(c) Other people back off when they slap their own head.

(d) The sensations arising from the endorphins this action produces are pleasurable.

If this person also has a limited repertoire of skills due to the impact of autism on their capacity to learn new skills, it is likely that they have an equally restricted range of behaviour choices. Consequently, this behaviour has become deeply embedded because the person has limited options for behaviour and has found that head-slapping effectively addresses a number of different needs. For people trying to understand the needs of an individual displaying challenging behaviour this **multi-functional** characteristic of many behaviour patterns is particularly difficult.

A further factor which can obscure attempts to effectively identify the need driving the challenging behaviour relates to the **shifting function** of behaviour over time. This is not an uncommon feature in the domain of challenging behaviour and can exist across a number of different time-frames, as demonstrated in Table 2.2. For example, a child may begin to push other children in order to obtain a favourite toy. Within a few days the child notices that whenever he pushes another child, people come rushing towards him which is very exciting and stimulating. Over a number of weeks, the child learns that after he has pushed a child, he is moved to a quiet play area with one adult who plays exclusively with him. The child eventually learns that whenever he pushes another child he is taken away from a noisy or challenging location to a quieter, safer place. At each stage of the evolution of this pushing behaviour, a different category of need has driven the behaviour. Consequently, the adults around the child may all hold differing opinions about the function of the behaviour which are related to the period of time in the behaviour's evolution that they are focusing on.

Sometimes this functional shifting occurs over a much shorter period. For example, an individual may begin screaming in order to gain attention, find that the demands being placed on them as they started to scream are withdrawn, recognise the stimulating sensations of loud noise and breathlessness and finally notice that the drink they receive to calm them down tastes very nice.

These two scenarios share a common characteristic in portraying a complex and shifting background in the function of behaviour. In these situations, people supporting individuals who exhibit challenging behaviour need to consider:

1 How behaviour patterns may have emerged originally.

2 Which category of need is maintaining the behaviour.

By aligning these two perspectives, it may be possible to identify strategies which enable the individual exhibiting the behaviour to acquire more appropriate means for meeting their needs.

This complex nature of needs analysis can be approached in two ways – namely:

■ Objectively

■ Subjectively.

Table 2.2 Changes in the function of behaviour over time

TIME

Pushing other children

Time	0–1 week	1–3 weeks	4–6 weeks	6–10 weeks	
Need	Tangible	Sensory	Attention	Escape	
Intent	To obtain a favourite toy	To stimulate excitement	To secure interaction with another person	To get away from noisy, frenetic environments	

Loud screaming

Time	0–1 minute	1–2 minutes	2–4 minutes	4–8 minutes
Need	Attention	Escape	Sensory	Tangible
Intent	To gain adult's attention	To avoid demands	To create exciting sensations	To obtain a drink

The first of these involves assessing the possible sources of challenging behaviour using a schedule or procedure which has been devised for this purpose. An example of this is the **Motivation Assessment Scale** devised by Durand and Crimmins (1992) which focuses on the four categories of need from which an individual's behaviour emerges.

The Motivation Assessment Scale is completed by a person or group of people who support an individual with challenging behaviour and analyses an identified behaviour and the conditions under which that behaviour occurs. Respondents are asked to rate sixteen items by selecting from seven possible descriptions of how often an individual would be expected to engage in the identified behaviour in a given situation. For example, people are asked a question such as:

Does the behaviour occur whenever you stop attending to this person?

and seven possible response ranging from 'never' through to 'seldom' to 'usually' and 'always' are provided. Having completed the schedule, responses are categorised around the four areas of sensory, escape, attention and tangible. A score is calculated according to the response rate recorded and a mean score for each category is provided. From this mean, the four areas are ranked according to the influence of a particular area of need on the individual's behaviour.

Following this needs-led analysis, a hypothesis can be formed around the likely cause of the behaviour, leading to the development of strategies which support alternative ways of addressing the individual's needs. Often, parents and practitioners have well-developed concepts of the likely causes of any challenging behaviour they are encountering. However, the benefits of using an instrument such as the Motivation Assessment Scale is that it introduces an element of **objectivity** to the process of needs analysis and enables the discussion related to an individual's challenging behaviour to be broadened to a wider audience for advice. Further information on the Motivation Assessment Scale, along with an on-line version of this instrument, can be found at www.monacoassociates.com.

Case Study: A lesson learned

I had been teaching Callum for over two years. He was a complex young boy with a diagnosis of autism compounded by severe learning difficulties. He also presented a range of challenging behaviours one of which involved ripping reading books if left unsupervised.

I was a comparatively experienced classroom practitioner and felt I knew Callum well. I considered the book-ripping to be an attention-gaining strategy as Callum would often gleefully giggle as he tore into the books and seemed to relish any fuss which his actions caused. In response to this perception I devised a number of behaviour support programmes focused around this need.

These programmes repeatedly failed and so I employed the Motivation Assessment Scale (MAS) to see if it could throw any light on the issue for me. To my surprise (and with hindsight, embarrassment!) the MAS identified sensory needs as the predominant issue in Callum's book-ripping. Armed with this new insight I designed a series of programmes focused on meeting these sensory needs such as providing Callum with a rucksack of old newspapers which he could rip whenever he had finished appointed tasks. Not only did this approach dramatically reduce the incidence of inappropriate ripping, it provided a highly motivating activity which could be offered as a reward to Callum for good work.

The second course of action which might be chosen involves listening to the opinions and ideas of people closely involved with the individual. This approach is **subjective** and is based on personal intuition and understanding of the individual being supported. It is important to remain cautious when using this approach and to prevent ideas with no basis in fact or whimsical, ill-informed notions to take hold of the process. However, the insights of families and 'front-line' practitioners, drawn from experience of and commitment to particular individuals, provide an invaluable resource in understanding the function of challenging behaviour.

In adopting this course of action, those people involved in supporting a person who exhibits challenging behaviour need to work in close, honest and open collaboration with one another. There need to be frequent, regular meetings which focus tightly on the behaviour causing concern and promote solutions to the difficulties all parties experience. These meetings should be rigorously documented and where possible take account of the views and wishes of the individual who displays challenging behaviour.

Identifying the needs which drive challenging behaviour is a complex and often frustrating exercise. People supporting individuals with autism and challenging behaviour may well benefit from combining both objective and subjective approaches in order to gain a comprehensive and holistic understanding of the individual's patterns of need.

Key points

- Behaviour support promotes positive behaviour.
- Human behaviour is a function of the context in which it occurs. Effective behaviour support relies on an effective functional analysis of that context.
- A person's behaviour is driven by need. Needs can be grouped into four broad categories, namely

  1 Attention

  2 Tangible

  3 Escape

  4 Sensory.

- Behaviour has a communicative purpose or intent.
- A single behaviour may fulfil several functions.
- The function of behaviour may alter over time.
- Objective and subjective approaches to understanding behaviour can be combined to provide a holistic and comprehensive view.

Chapter 3

Developing Proactive Strategies

> This chapter includes:
>
> - a definition of proactive strategies
> - a discussion of the optimum conditions for implementing proactive strategies
> - a number of strategies to promote optimum learning conditions.

Proactive strategies

Proactive strategies involve the deliberate engagement of positive and ethically sound interventions which are designed to pre-empt the occurrence of challenging behaviour. As previously discussed, proactive strategies must be based upon an effective analysis of an individual's needs and must enhance the life of the individual for whom the intervention has been designed.

Proactive strategies require those people supporting individuals who exhibit challenging behaviour to combine their 'scientific', empirical understanding of the function of an individual's behaviour with a creative flair for generating plausible solutions to apparently intractable problems. It is important to remember throughout this process, that the introduction of proactive strategies will inevitably create a new array of behaviour patterns. This is the consequence of the dynamic relationship between behaviour and the context it operates within. Any change introduced into the context will bring about a change in behaviour. This natural occurrence may be positive or negative and may produce behaviour which is either more appropriate or more challenging. Effective behaviour support generates new repertoires of behaviour which enable an individual to secure their needs without recourse to challenging episodes of behaviour.

Case Study: Jamal

Jamal's story presents a typical type of dilemma faced by classroom practitioners every day. Jamal was nine years old. A big boy for his age, he was prone to violent outbursts when demands were placed on him and the severity of these outbursts seemed to be increasing.

At a meeting to discuss these difficulties it was suggested that Jamal needed to learn more appropriate ways of avoiding demands and securing his favourite activities. It was proposed that Jamal be taught to pass a 'break symbol' to his teacher whenever he wanted to opt out of a work demand. This suggestion was based on the premise that Jamal had little control over what happened to him and little understanding of how he might secure his wishes.

However, this presented the group with an ethical and practical problem. Was it right, and was it sustainable, to let Jamal 'get his own way' all the time. Was this good for him? Was it fair on the other pupils around him? The group concluded that it was not; nor was the current situation tenable. As things stood, Jamal was avoiding work demands anyway by becoming violent and was dictating the structure of his school day in a negative spiral of causal events.

Consequently, a way of working needed to emerge which enabled Jamal to make meaningful decisions about his school day and allow him a measure of control over events without allowing him to dominate the situation. Therefore interventions were adopted which were **time limited** and which were seen as the first steps in a longer process of empowering Jamal and protecting the rights of those around him.

In the first instance, Jamal was to be taught how to operate the break symbol system. For a period of one month, the system would work consistently for him. Each time he asked to leave a situation he would be granted his request. At the same time, Jamal would be taught to tolerate waiting for a favourite item for gradually increasing periods, building from five seconds, to ten seconds and so on up to one minute. This would be done by presenting the item and counting audibly before handing it over. If Jamal behaved inappropriately, the item would be withdrawn; if he behaved appropriately, it would be handed to him.

Alongside this work, Jamal was also taught how to understand a simple reward system. Each time he behaved appropriately during work demands he would be given one of his favourite stickers. When he had ten stickers, he could go out to play on the climbing frame for five minutes.

After one month the situation was reviewed and it was agreed that the number and severity of attacks had reduced. The group decided that the break symbol system could be modified so that for a period of one more month, each time Jamal requested a break he would be asked to wait for one minute before he was allowed to leave the work situation. If he waited appropriately for the one-minute period, he was given a sticker.

This initiative worked successfully and the strategy was developed further. The new phase involved the teacher showing Jamal that he would be allowed a break after three defined activities had been completed. Jamal was rewarded with a sticker at the end of each activity and asked to wait one minute before he was allowed his 'break'. This structure was gradually built upon over the course of the school year so that eventually Jamal was able to tolerate prolonged periods of demand during the day knowing that he would be allowed a break from those demands at specified and secure periods.

Essentially, proactive strategies build upon an individual's capacity to learn. In this sense, learning may be understood as a process through which skills, knowledge and understanding are altered. Similarly, teaching might be regarded as intervention designed to alter a person's skills, knowledge and understanding. Teaching and learning are intricately related behaviours, each one acting upon the other in a continuously developing dyad of intervention and alteration. Consequently, effective proactive strategies are not static, universal programmes but constantly evolving and highly individualised interventions. Proactive strategies must be focused on the specific needs of an individual in a particular context and written in response to an assessment of those needs as a function of the context.

As a learning experience, the design of any proactive strategy must consider the **optimum learning conditions** which can be engineered in order to support an individual through the process. While a person might have specific, 'bespoke' optimum conditions for learning, there are a number of generally accepted prerequisites for learning which apply to the majority of people. These include

- a safe, healthy and calm learning environment

and

- relevant and motivating learning content.

Securing these basic prerequisites is critically important before any productive and positive learning can occur (see Chapter 5, 'Developing the Learning Environment').

However, people who exhibit challenging behaviour, almost by definition, are not easily able to access these setting conditions. For people who experience autism and display challenging behaviour, this problem is further compounded as a powerful series of circumstances act against the development of optimum learning conditions and the subsequent design of proactive strategies. Yet, as we have previously indicated, there is a moral obligation to act and action requires proactive strategies.

The key issue for people supporting individuals with autism and challenging behaviour is the timing of interventions especially those interventions which involve proactive strategies. As far as is possible, optimum learning conditions must be secured in order for proactive interventions to be effective. Identifying the circumstances under which these conditions are achievable is the key to successful intervention.

Case Study: Simon

Simon was twelve years old, a bright and articulate youngster with a passionate interest in several areas of learning and obdurate resistance to several others. He attended a large secondary school which served his neighbourhood and while his first few months in the school had been positive, concerns were growing as his resistance to certain subjects was now becoming manifest in negative ways. He would arrive late for certain lessons and often behave inappropriately throughout, disrupting other pupils or refusing to complete learning tasks.

People working with Simon found it difficult to determine why some areas of the curriculum were motivating for him and others were not. His interests did not seem to be subject oriented nor related to the people who taught those subjects. Eventually, colleagues began to consider whether or not it was to do with the location of classrooms as his behaviour was often associated with a particular block within the school campus.

Over time discussions with Simon revealed that he found the transition to this particular part of the school very difficult as he had to cross a large area where older pupils congregated and while there was no overt evidence of bullying, Simon clearly felt intimidated by this group. He was often late for class because he was waiting for the older pupils to disperse and when he did eventually arrive he was often tense and defensive.

Consequently, the staff team set about devising ways in which this transition could become less stressful for Simon. Initially, a member of staff was designated to accompany Simon and several other classmates across to the particular learning block. This was to enable Simon to cross the 'difficult area' securely without being singled out as he was within a group. It was then decided to organise the group to transit without a member of staff but ensuring all the pupils were present before they set off from their base.

Eventually, Simon was asked to co-ordinate this group of pupils which gave him a directed purpose and enabled him to focus on the logistics of moving the group rather than the possibility of issues with older pupils.

Introducing proactive strategies

The development of proactive strategies is a complex and highly demanding area of practice. Crucially, the effective engagement of proactive strategies depends upon the people supporting individuals with autism and challenging behaviour, identifying periods of time when the individual is sufficiently calm and focused in order to benefit from proactive intervention. This process can be facilitated by understanding human behaviour as driven by a continuous flow of emotional states which are, at times, excited or agitated and at other times calm and steady. Throughout the course of every day, each of us experiences events or episodes which stimulate or regulate our emotional state. This in turn affects our behaviour and causes us to act in particular and identifiable ways. This continuous flow can be shown as a line on a graph of arousal against time. Challenging behaviour can be seen to occur at those peaks in the graph when the levels of arousal are high. The introduction of proactive strategies is most effective during the periods of extended low level arousal. This concept is illustrated in Figures 3.1 and 3.2.

It is a useful exercise to place ourselves within this framework and evaluate the flow of our emotional states over the course of an average day. For example, we might wake up feeling refreshed and rejuvenated after a good night's sleep. We get dressed, eat breakfast and set off for work. The journey to work is comparatively smooth until the last mile or so when the traffic is inexplicably heavy and we start to worry about being late.

The traffic clears and we arrive on time and settle down to a productive morning. Midway through the morning we hear that our manager has been impressed by the work we are doing and wants to speak with us later in the day. Gradually we become excited as we imagine the possibility of a promotion or a pay rise. The manager calls us into the office, praises us and thanks us but nothing more. Mildly disappointed we return to our work.

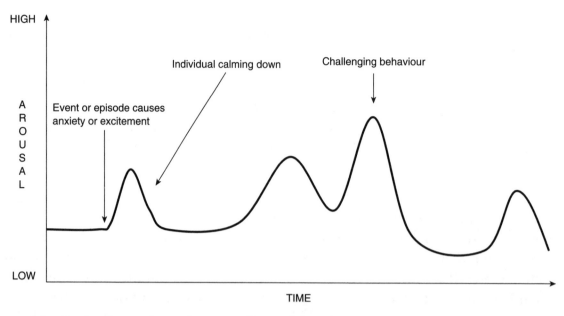

Figure 3.1   Levels of arousal over time caused by anxiety or excitement

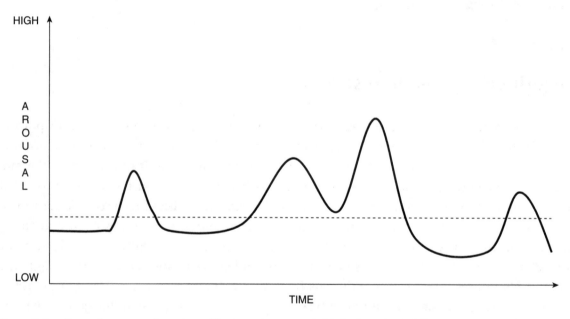

Figure 3.2   Proactive strategies most effective when arousal is below dotted line

No sooner are we back on task than a potential crisis looms. We realise we have forgotten to complete an important piece of work we had promised to finish by the end of the day. We quickly kick into action and work furiously through the lunch break just about completing the task before the deadline. Tired but relieved to have saved the day we travel home and settle down to an evening in front of the television.

Just as we relaxing, we get a call from a friend who has broken down about a mile from home and needs a lift to get home. The weather has turned foul so we hurry to get ready and drive out to meet them. We pick them up, drop them off and return home to finally sink into the sofa.

Plotting these events against the graphs shown above, it is possible to identify those points at which the capacity to absorb new information becomes compromised by the heightened state

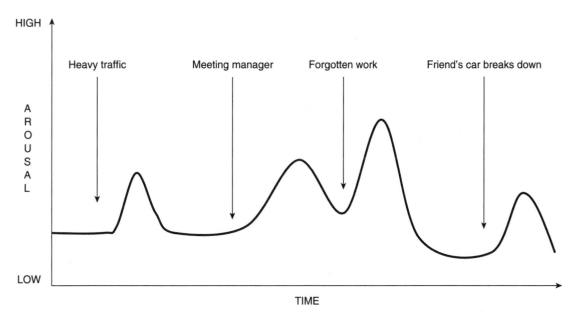

Figure 3.3   The 'average day'

of arousal (see Figure 3.3). Even when arousal is raised by potentially pleasant prospects, the ability to concentrate on the task in hand is diminished. Equally, the frenetic activity caused by the unfinished task does not constitute learning; it is possible to be industrious without acquiring any new skills or knowledge and possible to appear passive while learning a significant amount.

Appreciating the rises and falls in our arousal levels over time enables us to transfer this understanding to the experiences of people with autism. While for the most part, the majority of people without autism are able to cope with the increased pressures of heightened arousal, people with autism may well find the peaks of arousal extremely difficult to manage. Consequently, these heightened levels may disable the person's ability to process information and create a vortex of confusion and fear. Challenging behaviour may well occur at these points.

A further compounding factor which must be incorporated into our understanding of this model of human behaviour is the fact that many people with autism experience a heightened level of arousal for much of the time. This may be the result of anxiety which arises from difficulties in interpreting and processing a range of information and stimuli. Alternatively, excitement may be exaggerated by the extreme sensitivity to sensory stimuli many people with autism experience or the prospect of engaging in obsessive activities.

One consequence of this persistent level of heightened arousal is that people with autism may experience higher peaks of excited or agitated behaviour. This entails that people with autism may veer towards 'crisis' more easily than people without autism. A further consequence of prolonged heightened arousal is that many people with autism are often extremely fatigued. This almost permanent exhaustion decreases a person's tolerance levels, making them more liable to outbursts. This further exacerbates the problem as a vicious cycle of high anxiety, exhaustion and outburst creating higher levels of anxiety quickly develops.

If we explore this feature of autism and challenging behaviour graphically, it may look something like Figure 3.4. In this illustration a scale has been introduced to the level of arousal in

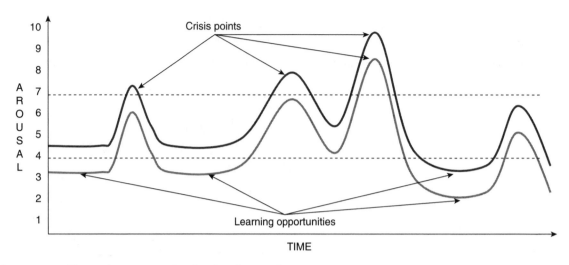

Figure 3.4   Illustration comparing levels of arousal

order to compare the opportunities for proactive interventions being engaged and the possibilities of crisis being reached.

In Figure 3.4 the darker line represents the levels of arousal experienced by a person with autism and the lighter line those experienced by a person without autism. Crucially, the ebb and flow of emotional states is described along the same profile. However, the starting points for levels of arousal are different. If it is assumed that point 4 on the arousal scale is the point below which productive learning might occur and point 7 is the point above which crises may occur, a stark fact becomes evident. In this specific example, the person with autism experiences three points of crisis while the person without autism experiences one. Equally the person without autism experiences three periods during which learning may be most effective while the person with autism experiences just one. If we measure these phenomena in terms of time, the person with autism spends more time approaching, or at, crisis point than they experience quality opportunities for learning.

It should be noted that Figure 3.4 is purely an illustrative exercise designed to highlight the possible differences between the levels of arousal experienced by people with autism. It is not an empirically based statement but rather a general indicator of the higher levels of stress and tension many people with autism encounter day after day. For those people supporting individuals with autism and challenging behaviour the identification of periods during which proactive interventions might be most effective is clearly complex and uncertain. The following exercise and resources are intended to support this process.

In order to identify periods when proactive interventions might be most effective for a person with autism and challenging behaviour it is helpful to collect data from structured observations of individuals. Data based on behavioural observations may present several critical pieces of information by:

1   Revealing a time-related pattern of calm and focused behaviour.

2   Indicating possible precursors to episodes of challenging behaviour.

3   Quantifying the length of time an individual can focus effectively.

Clearly, these behavioural observations are based solely on the outward activity of an individual and are only a secondary source of information about physiological, psychological and emotional factors. However, they are the only basis most people supporting individuals with autism and challenging behaviour have to work from and as such can be particularly valuable.

It is important to structure observations in order to produce information which is reliable and useful. Invariably, the process requires several weeks of observation, discussion and analysis and generally benefits from a clear statement of intent from the outset. Figures 3.5 and 3.6 provide an example of how the observation process might be structured around a common format. This enables a significant amount of data to be condensed into a single space which supports the interpretation and analysis of the data.

In this example, the process is followed through one morning during the observation period and shows how the blank format is completed to describe child J's observable behaviour.

Figure 3.5 is a blank sheet which depicts time set at fifteen-minute intervals across one axis and a scale of arousal from 1 to 10 across the other. People supporting individuals with challenging behaviour might choose to set the time differentials at any intervals which are appropriate to the context they are operating in. Consequently, intervals may be every thirty seconds or every hour or even every day.

Similarly, while the vertical axis in Figure 3.5 is calibrated from 1 to 10, any scale of numbers may be adopted to allow a range of interpretive positions to be adopted. Again the value of 4 has been indicated as the level below which proactive strategies may be gainfully employed and 7 as the level above which crises may occur. While not entirely arbitrary, this is not an empirically informed choice and other people may choose to re-set these values according to the situations they are analysing.

Figure 3.6 depicts the process of plotting observed behaviour onto the format and connecting each point with a line in order to depict the flow of arousal over the period examined. It is important to remember at this point that autism is a behaviourally defined condition and therefore open to subjective interpretations. Consequently, it is vital that claims for the validity and reliability of the data collected throughout this process are limited and circumspect.

The commentary may, over time, provide a pattern of behaviour related to predictable events. In the example given, perhaps break time presents J. with a challenge due to the demands of mixing with large groups of children in an unstructured environment. Alternatively, perhaps J. needs to consistently complete each task thoroughly before he can be moved on to the next set of activities. Examining the data over a number of days or weeks may determine which of these factors is salient.

In terms of developing proactive strategies and identifying those times when these may be most effectively engaged, Figure 3.6 provides several important insights. Firstly, a pattern of behaviour may emerge which can be associated with J. calming down towards a level of arousal at which proactive strategies may be effective. This may be interpreted in two ways – namely, does the behaviour pattern signal a reduction in arousal or does it actively work to calm J. down. Either way, the conditions around the calming procedure can be replicated in order to provide support to the process of securing the optimum learning conditions for J.

Proactive Intervention – Observation Sheet (Blank)

	09:00	09:15	09:30	09:45	10:00	10:15	10:30	10:45	11:00	11:15	11:30	11:45	12:00	12:15	12:30
10															
9															
8															
7															
6															
5															
4															
3															
2															
1															
COMMENTS															

Figure 3.5   Proactive Intervention – Observation Sheet (Blank)

Positive Behaviour Strategies to Support Children and Young People with Autism,
Paul Chapman Publishing © Martin Hanbury, 2007

Proactive Intervention – Observation Sheet – Exemplar Curve

	09:00	09:15	09:30	09:45	10:00	10:15	10:30	10:45	11:00	11:15	11:30	11:45	12:00	12:15	12:30
COMMENTS	J. upset on entry to school	Library base	Mrs G. offers drink – 'no thank you'	Reading alone	Number work – stickers for reward	Working well until break time	Outburst – wanted to finish work but break time	Inside during break / Tearful	Quiet – asking for drink	Good work – asking to work with P.	Working with P. Literacy	Calm – good working	Asking for dinner / Requests sitting alone	Mrs G. directs J. to dining hall	Sitting in dining hall / Hand-flapping

Figure 3.6   Proactive Intervention – Observation Sheet – Exemplar Curve

Positive Behaviour Strategies to Support Children and Young People with Autism,
Paul Chapman Publishing © Martin Hanbury, 2007

Case Study: Sarah

Sarah was a Key Stage 2 pupil who enjoyed positive and productive relationships with the teachers and teaching assistants she worked with. Yet there seemed to be periods during the day when Sarah's behaviour became extremely challenging. During these episodes Sarah presented a risk to both herself and people around her and, over time, the people supporting Sarah decided that during these episodes a minimal demand environment needed to be established around her.

However, colleagues were not clear on whether there were identifiable factors causing these behaviour outbursts and began to collect data on the outbursts using data collection instruments such as those presented in Figures 3.5 and 3.6, and in Table 3.1 on page 32. This process provided no insights into the causes of behaviour but it very quickly revealed a time patterning around the challenging episodes.

Consequently, the team supporting Sarah were able to predict with a reasonable degree of accuracy, those portions of the school day when Sarah was more likely to be receptive to learning activities. Accordingly, her timetable was altered to 'load' those periods when she was receptive with high demand learning tasks and 'lighten' those periods when Sarah tended to be more challenging. The team were therefore able to avoid exacerbating difficult time periods and capitalise on positive and productive periods.

Clearing a space for learning

As we have previously discussed, effective learning is most likely to occur when an individual's level of excitement or agitation is contained within certain limits. For people with autism, these states of arousal may be persistently exaggerated due to the nature of their condition which causes them to be prone to excitement or agitation. This comparatively heightened state of arousal is shown in Figure 3.4. In order to enhance opportunities for introducing proactive strategies, approaches directed at reducing the overall level of arousal can be extremely beneficial. This process may be seen as clearing a space for learning to occur, learning which will significantly improve the quality of the individual's life. Uniquely, strategies employed for clearing a space for learning may simultaneously be considered as proactive strategies and as the prerequisite groundwork which enables the engagement of proactive strategies. This duality is a critical feature of this element of behaviour support.

Before considering which approaches might be most effective, it is necessary to discuss the role of **medical intervention** in this regard. This is an area which is ethically complex and does not accommodate definitive or absolute positions.

It is undoubtedly the case that in the past medical intervention has been used inappropriately in the management of challenging behaviour. Individuals with autism and challenging behaviour have been subjected to a range of questionable surgical procedures and chemical interventions whose benefits could not be proven. Whatever the possible good intentions of those who implemented these misguided approaches, we are now in a position to dismiss as unethical any intervention which is not entirely focused on the needs and best interests of the person who is subjected to that intervention.

However, just as there is a place for medical intervention in the lives of any person, so too there is a place for medical intervention in the lives of people with autism and challenging behaviour. For example, if a person suffers from severe anxiety and panic attacks, the most appropriate treatment for their condition at a given point in time, may well be pharmacologically based. If a person has autism, there is no reason why their mental health needs should be any less than any other person and equally no reason why their entitlement to medical assistance in whatever form should be any less. Equally, the use of any medical intervention must be entirely determined on the basis of the best interests of the person who the intervention is prescribed for. There are no circumstances in which medical intervention can be ethically justified on the grounds that it reduces the challenge of behaviour to other people.

Naturally, judging what the best interests of an individual are, particularly if that individual's ability to speak for themselves is limited, is problematic. The rights of individuals with autism and challenging behaviour are paramount and in order to secure these rights it is vital that all parties directly involved in the care and protection of an individual maintain regular, collaborative practice across all aspects of that person's life. In this way, the interests of the person with autism can be protected and continuously reviewed.

Alongside, or as an alternative to medical intervention, individuals with autism and challenging behaviour may benefit from parallel approaches to reducing the levels of arousal they experience. The first of these involves offering **improved lifestyle options** for the individual with autism which serve to decrease the overall 'background' of arousal which affects their interaction with the world.

Improved lifestyle options tend to be long-term and slow-acting responses which gradually work to lower the overall level of anxiety or excitement a person generally experiences. Examples of these strategies fall into six broad categories – namely:

- Diet
- Health
- Leisure
- Self-advocacy
- Sensory support
- Skills and knowledge

which can be associated with improving the lifestyle of anyone in any context. For people with autism and challenging behaviour, it is often necessary for those people who support them to introduce the lifestyle changes that most individuals ordinarily make for themselves. These changes can be brought about by evaluating the lifestyle options available to the person with autism and then considering how each of these might be improved. These improvements might then be phrased as a set of learning objectives with the primary purpose of reducing levels of anxiety or excitement. Table 3.1 provides an example of a resource which might support this approach.

Table 3.1 Improving Lifestyle Options – Evaluation Schedule

Diet	Health	Leisure	Self-advocacy	Sensory support	Skills
What is the current situation?					
Limited to pasta, rice, bread	Generally good apart from stomach pain

Some problems with dental care | Limited engagement with leisure activities – watches cartoons on TV | Language use limited to 2/3-word phrases

Difficulties in expressing emotions | D. becomes very agitated when L. becomes distressed – possibly sensitive to high-pitched crying | Self-help skills limited – cannot clean teeth and is reluctant to let others help |
| **What can be done to improve this situation?** | | | | | |
| Introduce other food groups – one item from each group per month | See note on Diet
See note on Skills | Introduce visits to cinema

Teach D. to use DVD player to watch variety of cartoons | Focus on use of symbols to express emotions | Encourage D. to use his MP3 player when L. is becoming upset

Teach D. to ask for MP3 player | Introduce teeth-brushing programme during the next month |
| **What is the intended outcome?** | | | | | |
| Reduction in stomach pain

Enjoyment of broader range of foods | Reduction in stomach pain | Accessing public amenities

Develop independence in using leisure equipment | D. will be able to inform others how he is feeling and whether suggested activity appeals to him | D. will be able to use his MP3 player to distract him from high-pitched noises | D. will be able to clean his own teeth thereby reducing conflict with staff over teeth-cleaning routine |

Positive Behaviour Strategies to Support Children and Young People with Autism,
Paul Chapman Publishing © Martin Hanbury, 2007

By considering the various components of an individual's lifestyle as discrete entities it is possible to identify concrete strategies which combined into an integrated approach can significantly improve a person's lifestyle. Crucially, improving lifestyle options empowers an individual and enables them to feel more in control of their lives. Consequently, the levels of tension, frustration and confusion an individual experiences can be substantially reduced. Lizzie's story is a practical example of lifestyle improvement strategies enhancing the quality of a person's life.

Case Study: Lizzie

Lizzie was a 22-year-old woman who had recently moved into a shared house supported by 3 members of staff on a 24-hour basis. Lizzie experienced severe learning difficulties, epilepsy and autism, used no recognisable verbal language and displayed episodes of self-injurious behaviour when distressed. She was a highly dependent young woman supported by a skilled and committed team of people who gradually introduced a series of approaches which significantly improved the quality of Lizzie's life.

The first of these was medically based as the team collaborated with healthcare professionals to alleviate the menstrual difficulties Lizzie suffered. This involved acquiring data over a number of months which enabled the doctors to prescribe appropriate medication.

Once this dimension of difficulty had been eased, the team concentrated on improving Lizzie's diet. Lizzie had entered the house with a diet which was limited to foods which were largely unhealthy due to high sugar and fat content and significant amounts of additives and stimulants. The addictive nature of this diet coupled with Lizzie's inability to identify when she was 'full' entailed that she had a tendency to gorge on foodstuffs and had become overweight. This had begun to restrict her access to physical activity and resulted in periods of distress if she was required to walk any distance.

Consequently, advice was sought from a nutritionist and an exercise programme was devised which gradually increased the physical demands placed on Lizzie. These two initiatives enabled Lizzie to lose weight, establish a better sleeping routine and become generally more healthy.

The improvements in Lizzie's diet and general health enabled her to access a broader range of leisure activities including her favourite activity, swimming. This promoted a virtuous circle of exercise and enjoyment as Lizzie accessed swimming sessions three times a week.

Having provided an improved quality of life for Lizzie and introduced a sustained period of good health, the team were then able to begin teaching Lizzie a number of communication strategies. These enabled Lizzie to better advocate for herself and express her immediate needs and wishes. This progress allowed Lizzie to inform members of the team when her housemate's noises were upsetting her and therefore introduced some measure of sensory control into Lizzie's life.

This overall reduction in the tension experienced by Lizzie enabled the team to focus on the development of some basic life-skills for Lizzie, such as making a small snack or drink for herself. Lizzie, therefore, achieved some degree of independence and self-determination. In short, the quality of her life improved.

Improving lifestyle options introduces changes at a profound and enduring level. The process is necessarily slow and based on long-term perspectives and because of this the progress an individual is making is sometimes overlooked. This is why **longitudinal data** becomes important as it reflects the advances which are made on a steady, incremental basis. This in turn encourages both the individual with autism and challenging behaviour and those people who support the individual by enabling a focus on the positive long-term gains which are being made.

While improved lifestyle options offer an enduring approach to proactive strategies, there is invariably an urgent need to secure opportunities for proactive interventions in the short term. This second perspective to approaches can be seen in terms of **incident-specific strategies** which focus on supporting individuals during problematic day-to-day episodes. These strategies can be seen in terms of four broad categories – namely:

- Avoidance

- Calming techniques

- Distraction

- Options.

At any one time several strategies drawn from a number of these areas may be operating concurrently. People supporting individuals with autism and challenging behaviour need to ensure that these various strategies are complementary and sustainable. Strategies emerging from these four categories may be characterised as follows:

Avoidance

Avoiding difficult situations may be seen by some as 'giving in' to the challenging behaviour exhibited by an individual. However, when working with people with autism and challenging behaviour, the focus should always be on creating 'win–win' situations. Invariably, a person exhibits challenging behaviour because they have a fundamental difficulty which no amount of confrontation will resolve. Before provoking situations which are conflictual it is important to ascertain what is to be gained by the conflict. Naturally, there may be times when addressing the problem directly is the most ethical and pragmatic option. However, avoiding situations which agitate, over-stimulate or frighten individuals until such a time as the individual is better able to cope with the problem is invariably the best option.

What is critical in these circumstances is that avoidance is seen as a short term measure and not a long-term solution. Securing stability and success in the short term can lay the foundations for significant long-term gains achieved through improving lifestyle options via a concurrent group of approaches.

Case Study: Michael

Michael had always enjoyed horse riding. Despite a severely restricted vocabulary he had mastered the names of his favourite horses at the local stables and was always excited whenever he clambered aboard the minibus to head off to horse riding.

Riding represented a particularly positive element of Michael's life which was challenging in so many other ways. So it was very sad when, apparently with no warning and with no cause that anyone close to him could identify, Michael began to become very challenging whenever the group prepared to go horse riding.

His parents were very upset. This was the one area of his life that he seemed to enjoy and yet even this seemed to be taken from him. Consequently, the class teacher persevered in his efforts to take Michael horse riding until eventually, the risks to Michael and everyone around him became too great.

After consulting with Michael's family and colleagues within the school, the decision was taken to suspend Michael's horse-riding sessions until a clear idea could be formed around the possible sudden changes in his attitude towards riding.

For a period of half a term, Michael would be taken to play outside while the group prepared for horse riding. He would return to his class base after the other pupils had left and engage in one-to-one activities while the other pupils were out. This reduced the number of challenging episodes and seemed to improve Michael's behaviour in general. Data was collected and compared with previous data to reveal a significant reduction in challenging episodes once horse riding was taken off the timetable.

One possible explanation for this was that while Michael enjoyed horse riding, he found the increase in excitement and arousal levels associated with the sessions difficult to understand and integrate into his general perception of the world. As his awareness developed, he began to associate the class group's preparation for horse riding with the unpleasant feelings his overstimulated state gave him. Consequently, although the action of horse riding was enjoyable for Michael, the excitement that came with it was disorienting and unpleasant; his challenging behaviour may have been a result of this.

Allowing Michael a break from horse riding enabled the team of people supporting him to better understand the complex maelstrom of emotions Michael felt during and around horse-riding sessions. This 'time out' enabled the team to devise longer-term strategies which helped Michael identify his emotions and express 'opt out' choices appropriately. After several months of consolidated work in this area the team felt confident enough to re-present horse riding as an option to Michael knowing that he had the capacity to reject the session if he chose to. This empowered situation enabled Michael to return to the activity on a regular basis with the fall-back position of rejecting the session if he felt overstimulated by it.

Calming techniques

Every human being has a repertoire of individualised techniques which are used to calm and reassure. This range of approaches includes having a short break, talking to another person, talking to oneself, taking some exercise, controlling breathing or soothing the senses via approaches such as music or aromatherapy. This group of techniques are vital in enabling us to overcome the many tensions and pressures we face on a daily basis.

For people with autism and challenging behaviour, access to these critical components is extremely limited. This is often because people with autism and challenging behaviour are limited in their ability to appreciate the escalation of tension or agitation and are therefore unable to engage in calming techniques. Consequently, it is necessary for those people supporting the individual to establish a portfolio of techniques which can be introduced when circumstances dictate.

Invariably, these techniques are similar to those that all human beings use but must be carefully chosen to meet the needs of the individual. Teams of people supporting individuals must be cautious in their selection of techniques. For example, for many people with autism, their capacity to process language significantly diminishes under pressure and approaches based on calm and reassuring speech may be misguided. In difficult situations, the requirement to process language may be an added demand even for more able, linguistically competent people with autism. In addition to this consideration, some people with autism and challenging behaviour may find sensory input over-stimulating and experience increased levels of arousal which exacerbate situations. Consequently, it is necessary to carefully consider each technique which is introduced and to consult broadly in order to gather as much information around the individual as possible.

A further complication in developing calming techniques for individuals with autism and challenging behaviour arises because the people supporting the individual fail to recognise particular behaviour patterns as part of a self-generated calming routine. Consequently, the behaviour is perceived as an indicator of escalating tension rather than a self-initiated calming technique and the process is interrupted, leading to episodes of challenging behaviour. Therefore, it is important to ensure that teams of people supporting individuals do not over-react to certain elements of behaviour but try and ascertain the role each component of a given behaviour pattern is performing.

Case Study: Ria

Ria was a complex little girl who repeatedly surprised us, confounded us and amazed us. Throughout the two years she had attended school, she had proved to be unpredictable in many ways. Although she worked with established and highly skilled staff members and shared strong and caring relationships with these practitioners, her sudden mood swings were difficult to predict and they were beginning to limit her access to many places and activities.

The team supporting Ria met with her mum and dad and other professionals involved in her life and tried to identify the root causes of the behavioural difficulties Ria displayed. Unfortunately, the group were unable to successfully identify any consistent factors and concluded that the only consistent pattern was the complete lack of consistent pattern!

However, in the course of the conversation, it became apparent that people had evolved routines which they used to calm Ria whenever she was becoming agitated. These routines varied in their effectiveness but generally seemed to introduce some measure of stability into difficult situations and seemed to have a common thread which the group decided to try and focus on. The underlying premise was that if the group could not determine the causes of Ria's challenging behaviour, they needed at least to develop effective strategies for stabilising difficulties.

Discussions revealed that Ria seemed to benefit from a soothing song being sung to her whenever she was about to encounter a stressful situation. Staff in school had used this technique when Ria was being examined by the school nurse and her mum had used the strategy when she had taken Ria for a haircut.

However, the technique did not always work. For example, her mum noted that it rarely worked when she was outside and members of the school staff team agreed that the technique had no effect in the school playground. This factor was unfortunate because Ria was scared of dogs and the family had stopped visiting local parks because of this. Similarly, there were certain pupils Ria was wary of and their presence in the playground had provoked Ria to attack children and members of staff resulting in her access to the playground becoming more restricted.

The group were perplexed until someone offered the notion that perhaps people were singing more quietly in the enclosed space of the medical room and the hairdressers. From this the group speculated that perhaps it was the proximity of the adult to Ria and the sensation of the adult's warm breath near her that enabled her to become calm. As discussion developed it emerged that other techniques which had soothed Ria included people blowing softly on her head or whispering 'shh' into her ear.

Through the processes of discussion, through an honest and open discourse, the group had identified that the key factor for Ria was not the music but the warmth and close proximity of supportive adults. Calming techniques could now focus on employing these strategies whenever Ria was likely to encounter a stressful situation.

Distraction

Distraction techniques are used frequently by human beings to ease interactions and support positive relationships. They are commonly employed by the parents of young children who will draw the child's attention to a favourite toy or character while some less than pleasant procedure is completed. This might be anything from injections, to haircuts, to tasting new foodstuffs.

For individuals with autism and challenging behaviour the careful use of distraction techniques can be highly effective. Again people supporting the individual must be cautious in their use of these techniques, ensuring that they are not choosing a 'distractor' which serves only to worsen the situation. Experienced families and practitioners in this field are often found with small rucksacks full of tried and tested toys, books and gimmicks whose function is to draw an individual's attention away from problematic scenarios.

Other people supporting individuals with autism and challenging behaviour become adept at 'thinking on their feet', displaying a fine sensitivity for their surroundings and drawing upon objects or occurrences in the environment to draw an individual's focus away from potentially difficult stimuli.

Case Study: Junaid

Junaid had made the transition into Key Stage 2 very well. He had a creative and imaginative teacher and a talented and dedicated teaching assistant supporting every aspect of his school-life. His progress was good and crucially Junaid seemed to be very happy at school.

There remained, however, one area of concern – namely, assemblies. These had never been positive experiences for Junaid as he found it difficult to tolerate the large group, increased noise and what he considered to be the meaningless content of assemblies. Previously he had refused to enter the hall for assembly or presented significant challenges once in the hall and therefore had been removed from the situation. Consequently, the history and management of previous difficulties did not provide a good foundation for progress.

However, the team supporting Junaid wanted to move him on and felt that the progress he had made in so many other areas justified the attempt to gradually introduce him to assemblies. While it was a risk in some respects, it also represented a high expectation of Junaid and faith in his ability to learn.

It was recognised that in order to tolerate assemblies Junaid would need a series of distractions to enable him to overcome the negative associations he held. The initial objective of the team was to enable Junaid simply to spend increasing periods of time in the assembly with no emphasis on having to engage in the content of the assembly.

Consequently, it was decided that Junaid could take his favourite magazines and comics into the assembly and sit and read these at the back of the hall for the duration of the assembly. After a number of successes doing this the team decided to ask Junaid to sit at the end of the row reading his comics and gradually moved him further along the row over the subsequent weeks.

After a term and a half, Junaid was asked to take just one magazine into the assembly and after a further few months was asked to take the magazine into assembly but only begin reading it after three minutes had passed. This was gradually increased to five and then seven and then ten minutes. This incremental approach enabled Junaid to successfully join assemblies so that eventually he was able to carry a magazine into the hall and leave it by the hall door. Knowing that the magazine was there was a sufficient distraction to Junaid to support him in tolerating assemblies. He even started to enjoy some of them!

Options

Many people with autism and challenging behaviour have a sense of powerlessness. This is the result of many episodes in their lives during which control has been wrested from them as part of the management of their behaviour. This entails that some individuals may have very limited choices and equally limited self-esteem.

In some circumstances, individuals may passively accept certain conditions because they are 'conditioned' to do so. Often this causes challenging behaviour as their acquiescence suppresses their real desire to reject something which can only emerge following its imposition.

By increasing the available options to an individual, it is possible to reduce both the number of openly confrontational situations and the number of conflicts arising from the suppression of an individual's real feelings.

Case Study: Peter

Peter did not like wearing his coat. Most of the time this was not a major problem; sometimes it was, as Peter loved to be outdoors and in cold or wet weather he would insist on playing outdoors with no coat on and therefore be susceptible to colds and sore, chapped skin. Peter's family and the team working with him in school decided that a strategy needed developing otherwise Peter would be denied access to a range of his favourite activities.

After a long period of discussion and several meetings it was decided to present Peter with a number of choices of outdoor wear. Those people supporting him felt that if he could be encouraged to wear just a few more clothes when he played out, that this would serve as a foundation for enabling Peter to tolerate his coat.

A routine was gradually developed through which whenever Peter requested outside play, he would be presented with several items of clothing. When one item was chosen, Peter was given access to outside play.

Initially, Peter was very resistant to the new regime and presented several prolonged episodes of challenging behaviour in order to secure outside play without having to 'deal' for it. However, the people supporting him were calmly insistent, confident in the knowledge that in the longer term this approach was in Peter's best interests. Equally, they were prepared for the challenging episodes and were equipped and organised.

Eventually, Peter recognised that by agreeing to wear either a pair of gloves or a baseball cap or a thin sweatshirt he was gaining access to his favourite activities. Over time this choice was broadened to enable Peter to wear a greater range of suitable outdoor clothing. He continued to reject a coat, but he gradually wore more warm clothes in cold weather, a choice which has been accepted.

Figures 3.7–3.10 offer a number of suggestions to support the development of incident-specific strategies. The ideas explored here are drawn from experiences of successful strategies which have been employed in order to avoid crises. As previously indicated, one or more strategies may be engaged at any given time depending upon the nature of the difficulty being addressed. It is also possible to perceive particular interventions as belonging to several categories simultaneously.

Avoidance

Crowds: A person who finds large groups of people difficult will probably struggle in busy shopping centres, crowded stations, school assemblies or playgrounds and large celebrations. Desensitising an individual to the effect that large crowds have on them is a complex and long-term endeavour. In the short term, avoid these types of scenarios, introducing the individual to small groups and aiming for no more than a tolerance of these groups.

Eating: The heightened sensitivities of some individuals with autism determine that particular taste or olfactory sensations can be extremely aversive. This is not simply a case of dislike but rather a case of utter revulsion. While many parents or practitioners may be anxious to develop the dietary choices of an individual, it may be better to accept the limitations of an individual's diet rather than create an association between mealtimes and aversive experiences.

Relationships: Personality clashes are as likely to occur among individuals with autism as they are among anyone else. Indeed, the impairment in social understanding people with autism experience may exacerbate relationship problems. Where experience shows that certain individuals do not get on with one another, avoid placing these people together just as you might avoid meeting people you dislike yourself.

Figure 3.7   Strategies for supporting avoidance techniques

Calming techniques

Healthcare: Many people with autism have a history of unpleasant experiences in this area. Visits to the doctor, nurse or dentist may have terrifying connotations for individuals whose early life may have involved long and intrusive healthcare experiences. Prior to healthcare appointments, devise routines which promote a sense of calm reassurance for the individual. This may involve practising the route to the venue on the days leading up to the appointment, playing calming music, creating a social story related to the expected scenario, meeting the healthcare professional beforehand or simply holding a person's hand and offering soothing advice.

Public examinations: Many people become nervous prior to examinations and people with autism are as subject to this natural nervousness as anyone. Try and devise routines which 'talk' the individual through the examination process. Create a series of mental checklists for the individual which reassure the person that they have all the materials they need and have done a sufficient amount of work. Teach the individual breathing techniques which can be employed prior to entering the examination.

Trust: Many individuals with autism form special relationships with certain people who appear to offer security to the individual. Ensure that these 'trustees' are on hand whenever significant challenges are ahead for individuals.

Figure 3.8   Strategies for supporting calming techniques

Distraction

Phobias: Some phobias cannot be avoided while maintaining a reasonable quality of life. For example, if an individual is afraid of dogs, the only way they can avoid the inevitable encounter with a dog is to stay at home all the time, a prisoner of their phobia. In order to overcome this, plan a series of effective distraction techniques such as focusing a conversation on an individual's special interests, singing a familiar song or pointing out features of the environment. Have these techniques ready for use when outside the home environment.

Obsessions: Some individuals with autism and challenging behaviour have particular objects, routines, places or people they are obsessed with. When near these things the individual is likely to become excited and agitated and prone to episodes of challenging behaviour. People supporting the individual need to prepare for those times when proximity to an obsession is likely to be problematic. Devise strategies such as reminding the individual of a reward system which might be related to self-control or engage them in conversation about a favourite television programme.

Associations: Certain items, environments or people may remind individuals of unpleasant or exciting experiences. Prepare for these associations by devising interruptions to the association through conversations, word games, songs and rhymes.

Figure 3.9   Strategies for supporting distraction techniques

Options

Choosing who: There are certain unavoidable elements of a daily routine which may be difficult for an individual. For example, elements of personal care, mealtimes or journeys to and from school. While these things are necessary, it is possible to offer a choice of the person who supports the individual during these times. This gives some measure of empowerment to the individual and might serve to make the exercise more manageable.

Making decisions: The fundamental difficulty many people with autism encounter in the domain of **executive functioning** compromises the ability to make informed and balanced decisions. This may result in either apparently hasty and irrational choices or an inability to make a choice. Prepare individuals for making decisions by discussing the range of options available to them and gradually eliminating each one until a final choice is made. Alternatively, where individuals may not be able to achieve this, limit the number of choices available to avoid individuals becoming overwhelmed by choices.

Control: For individuals with autism and challenging behaviour, many aspects of their lives are beyond their control. Because of this, it is often important to identify one area of an individual's life in which they can enjoy total control. This may be in the choice of clothing they wear, programmes they watch or places they visit.

Figure 3.10   Strategies for increasing options

Table 3.2   Integrating incident-specific strategies and improved lifestyle options – example 1

Behavioural concern: H. becomes extremely agitated after evening visits from his mum finish. He does not settle well for his bedtime routine and as he gets more tired he becomes more violent towards members of staff and himself.

Avoidance	Calming techniques	Distraction	Options
1. Suggest afternoon visits from Mum for the next three months.	1. Introduce daily yoga programme scheduled to follow Mum's visits.	1. Immediately prior to Mum leaving, settle H. down to watch Thomas the Tank Engine.	1. H. to choose which member of staff works with him after Mum's visit.

Diet	Health	Self-advocacy	Leisure	Sensory support	Skills
1. Reduce all stimulants to support night-time routine.	1. Consult CAMHS* team to discuss support for separation anxieties.	1. Enable H. to reflect on his behaviour following Mum's visit using social stories. 2. Allow H. to select optimum time for visits.	1. Develop a range of leisure activities to promote relaxation such as yoga, aromatherapy, tai chi.	1. Develop quiet area for H. to enter whenever he feels agitated.	1. Teach H. to be able to express an increasingly broad range of choices using PECS**.

* Child and Adolescent Mental Health Services
** Picture Exchange Communication System

Table 3.3 Integrating incident-specific strategies and improved lifestyle options – example 2

Behavioural concern: K. is extremely passive during lessons. He refuses to contribute to discussions although his written work and one-to-one work show a clear understanding of the issues raised. K. is becoming increasingly introverted during lessons.

Avoidance	Calming techniques	Distraction	Options
1. Do not require K. to contribute to lessons. Praise his written and one-to-one work in an understated way.	1. Teach K. deep breathing techniques which he can use prior to and during lessons.	1. If K. seems agitated, encourage him to read course materials rather than engage with group.	1. Agree with K. two sessions during the term when he can make a prepared statement during lessons.

Diet	Health	Leisure	Self-advocacy	Sensory support	Skills
1. Offer K. access to drinks whenever he chooses during lessons.	1. Ensure K. does not have a headache during lessons. 2. You may need to ask him.	1. Encourage K. to join in one out-of-school activity in order to establish relationships.	1. Teach K. to indicate clearly and politely whether he is able to contribute to discussions.	1. Allow K. to stay in the library during playtimes.	1. Teach K. 'public speaking' skills on a private, one-to-one basis. 2. Offer rewards for entry into competition.

Table 3.4   Integrating incident-specific strategies and improved lifestyle options – example 3

Behavioural concern: S. becomes extremely excited every time she goes swimming. This often leads to challenging behaviour on arriving at the swimming pool, resulting in the staff at the leisure centre refusing to allow her to enter the pool.

Avoidance	Calming techniques	Distraction	Options
1. Arrange private swimming sessions outside public hours.	1. Offer S. favourite koosh ball when travelling to swimming baths. 2. Play 'Now 56' on journey.	1. On arriving at swimming baths ask S. to help carry swimming kits into changing area.	1. Offer S. choice of one of three swimming costumes.

Diet	Health	Leisure	Self-advocacy	Sensory support	Skills
1. Ensure S. eats at least two hours before swimming sessions.	1. Consolidate progress on continence training to increase confidence in this area.	1. Increase the range of facilities accessed at the leisure centre. 2. Join aerobics classes.	1. Teach S. to reject swimming as an activity using PECS*.	1. Provide regular and frequent access to water play outside scheduled swimming sessions.	1. Focus increasingly on learning to swim as opposed to water play.

* Picture Exchange Communication System

As indicated previously, the short-term nature of incident-specific strategies determines that they cannot secure long-term, life-enhancing qualities for an individual with autism and challenging behaviour. They are the behavioural equivalent of first aid in that they stabilise the problem and prevent it getting worse. But they do not offer a solution to the difficulties faced by individuals and, if left as the sole source of approaches, may eventually come to exacerbate the difficulties they were originally intended to address.

Equally, improving lifestyle options invariably requires many months of slow, steady work with limited progress over significant time-scales. Consequently, they cannot offer immediate support to individuals facing repeated crises. Their strength lies in the enduring quality of their effect and not in the capacity to resolve difficult daily occurrences.

Consequently, people supporting individuals with autism and challenging behaviour need to consider an **integrated approach** to intervention in which short-term measures and long-term solutions are strategically combined to secure both the immediate health and safety of individuals and their long term well-being and quality of life. Crucially, there needs to be a careful consideration of how short-term measures and long-term approaches are likely to interact with one another. This process should not paralyse support systems but should provide a sound rationale for every planned intervention. Tables 3.2–3.4 provide examples of how approaches may be designed to complement one another across short- and long-term perspectives.

The development of proactive strategies across both long- and short-term time-frames promotes a virtuous cycle of learning and lifestyle enhancement. This goal is the ultimate goal for all individuals with autism and challenging behaviour. However, it is difficult to attain, requiring patience, resilience, courage and a finely tuned analytical approach focused on the needs of the person with autism. If there is a genuine desire to improve the quality of life for any person with autism and challenging behaviour, then there needs to be a concerted and determined effort to introduce proactive strategies into their lives.

Key points

- Proactive strategies enable an individual to learn alternative ways to meet their needs.

- Proactive strategies build on an individual's capacity to learn and require optimum learning conditions.

- Identifying periods when an individual is calm is critical to the successful implementation of proactive strategies.

- Proactive strategies can be short-term or long-term.

- Improving a person's lifestyle options will promote optimum learning conditions.

- Identifying techniques which enable an individual to remain calm increases the likelihood of implementing effective proactive strategies.

- Proactive strategies both promote optimum learning conditions and can be implemented during optimum learning periods. This virtuous cycle is the aim of proactively supporting individuals with autism and challenging behaviour.

CHAPTER 4

Developing Our Role in Behaviour Support

This chapter includes:

- an examination of our role in behaviour support
- a discussion of the key qualities required to provide effective and enduring behaviour support
- an exploration of how organisations can further develop their capacity to support individuals.

Understanding ourselves

The processes of behaviour support are deeply enmeshed in the relationships shared by each person involved in those processes. People who support individuals with autism and challenging behaviour, whether they are family members or practitioners, are part of a dynamic and vibrant relationship in which every experience and interaction has an equally profound effect upon themselves and the individual they are supporting. Appreciating the fundamental role played by relationships is a critical feature of effective behaviour support. As relatives, friends or practitioners supporting individuals with autism and challenging behaviour, it is important to take some time to reflect on ourselves and the impact of our role in the complex and exciting relationship we share with that individual. In many respects, understanding ourselves is the first step in providing effective behaviour support to others.

Prior to developing approaches which support individuals with autism and challenging behaviour, a decision is made by those people who live or work with that individual that some degree of intervention is necessary. This decision is an ethical decision; it is based on a moral position adopted by the people around the individual that they are obliged to intervene in the life of another person in order to improve the quality of life that individual experiences. Undoubtedly there will be pragmatic considerations, legislative concerns and professional reasons for making this decision. But at its heart the decision is ethical, based on a person's concept of 'right action' and constructed from a unique complex of personal history and experience. Therefore, in order to better understand the processes that determine the development of behaviour support programmes, it is necessary to investigate the processes which affect our initial decision to intervene in the life of an individual.

Essentially, this complicated and deeply personal phenomenon involves a subjective judgement that the individual we are hoping to support does not enjoy the quality of life every human being is entitled to. In short, we intervene because we believe that the individual has a right to a better quality of life than the one we believe they experience. This notion of 'a good quality of life' is, of course, a personal construct and will naturally vary from person to person. What is a 'good life' for you may not necessarily be a 'good life' for me. There are, of course, certain parameters which most people would acknowledge reasonably describe a humane quality of life and which are enshrined in a number of internationally accepted laws and declarations, for example the Universal Declaration of Human Rights (United Nations, 1948) or the European Convention on Human Rights. Nonetheless, the pragmatic decision to intervene in the day-to-day life of another person begins with a subjective judgement based on our personal beliefs and values.

This being the case, we must acknowledge that whatever level of intervention we introduce we are likely to cause some degree of discomfort and stress to the individual. We are therefore morally bound to scrutinise the subjective judgements we are making and commit ourselves to a process of reflective self-examination in order to ensure the actions we are taking are focused on the individual's rights and best interests.

The questions we ask of ourselves at this point need to be rigorous and challenging and must drive at understanding our motives, our prejudices, our aspirations and our notions of normality. The process should not be an easy, self-affirming exercise but rather a challenging and at times uncomfortable quest to understand ourselves and our role in the dynamic we share with the individual we are hoping to support.

Initially we must ask ourselves:

What is it about this individual's quality of life that demands those of us supporting them make a conscious decision to intervene in order to affect change?

In order to answer this question satisfactorily each person offering support needs to have carefully considered their interpretation of the term 'quality of life'. This interpretation needs to be incorporated in our response to the question along with a description of the values which have led us to this view.

By addressing this issue, we are in a position to identify those features of the individual's life which significantly detract from their quality of life and demand our intervention.

Having established a rationale for intervention, we must then examine:

What is it about this individual's behaviour that causes me anxiety?

In answering this question we need to explore our own emotional, physiological and psychological responses to the individual's behaviour. From this, we may be able to proceed to an understanding of why we find the targeted behaviour difficult, to an acknowledgement of what factors from our own history and experiences cause us to react in the way we do to the behaviour.

This process can be particularly difficult and for some people can cause a re-awakening of fears and frailties they might have thought themselves to have overcome or left behind. However, supporting an individual with autism and challenging behaviour is an extremely demanding and challenging undertaking which requires us to draw on enormous reserves of inner strength and resolution. In respect to this element of our lives, those of us who take on this challenge need to be emotionally and psychologically robust and able to withstand the potentially upsetting process of introspection this exercise requires. Arguably, a person not equipped to undergo this self-examination may not be adequately equipped to offer enduring and sensitive support to an individual with autism and challenging behaviour.

Equally, relatives, colleagues and service managers need to recognise the fact that going through this process of introspection is difficult and that people prepared to engage in this exercise should be skilfully and sensitively supported.

A final element of this preliminary exercise in developing a programme of behaviour support for an individual requires a person to identify those qualities they bring to the process. We need to ask ourselves:

> *What qualities and characteristics can I offer to this process of intervention?*

For many people, this is an awkward question as they do not want to appear boastful or arrogant. However, this skills audit is as essential as the introspection required previously. In identifying our strengths and those attributes which will contribute positively to the behaviour support process, we will be able to determine the precise role we can play in the process and therefore strengthen the process.

This preliminary period of self-examination requires relatives, friends and practitioners who support individuals with autism and challenging behaviour to investigate the complex and deeply subjective judgements which are made when entering into the domain of behaviour support intervention. This difficult exercise might be clarified to some degree by using the schedule set out in Figure 4.1 in order to structure this introspection.

Owning challenging behaviour

Following this initial period of endeavouring to understand the effect of our histories and character on the interactions we share with individuals with challenging behaviour, it is important to attempt to develop an empathy with the individual with autism and challenging behaviour which extends to those periods of challenging behaviour we are trying to address.

This empathy is difficult to achieve in its entirety because people without autism can never fully appreciate what it is like to experience the condition. However, it is possible to move towards an empathy with individuals who have autism and display challenging behaviour because each of us engages in challenging behaviour to some degree at some time. Consequently, if we explore our own experiences of challenging behaviour, we may be better able to understand the challenging behaviour of other people.

People supporting individuals with autism and challenging behaviour might benefit from trying the following exercise. Complete Figure 4.2, focusing on your own behaviour and then duplicate the exercise for the person you are supporting by completing Figure 4.3.

This exercise requires the recognition that we are all capable of displaying challenging behaviour. For many people, this notion is difficult because they consider themselves reasonable and are able justify most of their actions within a rational framework. However, it is important to consider that from the point of view of any individual displaying challenging behaviour, their actions are reasonable and the world around them is unreasonable. In fact, we may go so far as to say that the challenging behaviour an individual with autism exhibits *is* a reasonable response to the context they experience given what we know about autism.

Section A

What is it about ....'s quality of life that demands I make a conscious decision to intervene in order to affect change?

1. The five things I value above anything else are

    ●

    ●

    ●

    ●

    ●

2. For all human beings a good quality of life must include

    ●

    ●

    ●

    ●

    ●

3. I believe ....'s life quality is significantly damaged by

    ●

    ●

    ●

    ●

    ●

Section B

What is it about this individual's behaviour that causes me anxiety?

1. How do I feel when ....' engages in this behaviour?

    ●

    ●

    ●

    ●

    ●

2. What physiological responses have I noticed in myself during episodes of this behaviour?

    ●

    ●

    ●

    ●

    ●

3. What factors from my previous experiences or current lifestyle may cause me to feel and respond in these ways?

-
-
-
-
-

Section C

What qualities and characteristics can I offer to this process of intervention?

1. What personal characteristics will enable me to provide effective behaviour support?

-
-
-
-
-

2. What skills, knowledge and understanding will support me in offering .... effective behaviour support?

-
-
-
-
-

3. What practical actions can I offer to support this intervention?

-
-
-
-
-

Figure 4.1   Self-examination schedule

**Positive Behaviour Strategies to Support Children and Young People with Autism,**
Paul Chapman Publishing © Martin Hanbury, 2007

1. Identify behaviour you have displayed which might be considered challenging by other people.

   [ ]

2. State why people might find this behaviour challenging.

   [ ]

3. Describe your emotional state when you are displaying this behaviour.

   [ ]

4. Identify why you display this behaviour.

   [ ]

5. Name the category of need you feel your behaviour emerges from.

Sensory	Escape	Attention	Tangible

6. Identify the alternatives to this behaviour you could adopt.

   [ ]

Figure 4.2   Developing Empathy: My Challenging Behaviour

Positive Behaviour Strategies to Support Children and Young People with Autism,
Paul Chapman Publishing © Martin Hanbury, 2007

1. Identify behaviour you consider to be challenging which is displayed by the individual you support.

2. State why you find this behaviour challenging.

3. Describe the apparent emotional state of the individual you support when they are displaying this behaviour.

4. Identify why you feel the individual displays this behaviour.

5. Name the category of need you feel this behaviour emerges from.

Sensory	Escape	Attention	Tangible

6. Identify the alternatives to this behaviour the individual is currently able to adopt.

Figure 4.3   Developing Empathy: Understanding Others

P **Positive Behaviour Strategies to Support Children and Young People with Autism,**
Paul Chapman Publishing © Martin Hanbury, 2007

Moving on, developing practice

The processes of understanding the role played by each person in the complex and unpredictable dynamics surrounding challenging behaviour are the first steps people supporting individuals with autism and challenging behaviour need to take. However, this introspection, while crucial, is not enough and families, friends and practitioners need to carefully consider the next dimension of self-development which needs to be engaged.

The first activity involves an accurate assessment of the skills and understanding which a person supporting an individual with challenging behaviour brings to the situation. These qualities can be understood across four broad categories – namely:

- Personal characteristics

- Physical attributes

- Theoretical understanding

- Practical experience.

In evaluating a person's strengths and needs across these categories, it is possible to identify particular areas which might be further developed for a person. It is only by honestly and accurately describing strengths and needs that people supporting individuals with autism and challenging behaviour can effectively improve the interventions and support they are able to offer that individual.

Personal characteristics

Any person supporting an individual with autism and challenging behaviour requires a prerequisite range of personal qualities which enables them to remain focused on the primary needs of the individual they are supporting. Crucially, these qualities need to be blended in order to ensure an appropriate balance of strength and sensitivity is achieved at all times. A person supporting an individual with autism and challenging behaviour needs to be able to draw upon qualities such as:

- Calmness – able to rationalise difficulties clearly

- Confidence – able to believe in themselves

- Conviction – believing in what they do

- Courage – some situations are likely to be dangerous

- Creativity – solutions will often be hidden

- Determination – not giving up when the going gets tough

- Empathy – able to perceive things as another person does

- Honesty – open and candid with themselves and others

- Humility – able to admit when mistakes have been made

- Initiative – thinking for themselves in adverse circumstances

- Resilience – able to sustain long periods of stress and anxiety

- Sympathy – caring enough to face highly stressful situations.

These qualities need to be a consistently recognisable part of a person's character with no one trait dominating others and all qualities remaining present in all situations.

Physical attributes

While it is not necessary to be an Olympic athlete to support people with autism and challenging behaviour there are certain physical traits which need to be present. This is because it is likely that at some point during the processes of support a person may have to draw upon some element of physical skill. People supporting individuals with autism and challenging behaviour need to be:

- Healthy – not carrying injuries or illness

- Fit – able to maintain physical activity for prolonged periods

- Co-ordinated – able to execute quick, precise movements

- Alert – able to spot danger and warn others

- Robust – have reasonable resources of strength and stamina.

Crucially, people supporting individuals with autism and challenging behaviour need to be physically competent and physically confident. Without these key attributes, people are vulnerable and increase the vulnerability of those around them.

Theoretical understanding

Autism is an infinitely complex condition presented across a broad spectrum of strengths and needs. It is a way of being which is difficult to understand and challenging to address. Equally challenging behaviour is the consequence of a series of problematic interactions between an individual and their environment. Its processes are often hidden and difficult to predict while solutions are invariably hard to identify. When these two conditions compound one another, they require the person supporting the individual with autism and challenging behaviour to draw upon a reserve of knowledge and understanding in order to try and extricate patterns and features which may help alleviate difficulties. Consequently, a good, thorough and up-to-date theoretical understanding of both autism and challenging behaviour provides the essential foundation to any effective processes of support. People supporting individuals with autism and challenging behaviour will benefit from a sound knowledge and practical understanding of:

- The triad of impairment (Wing, 1996)

- Theory of mind (Baron-Cohen, 1995)

- Executive function (Norman and Shallice, 1980)

- Central coherence theory (Frith, 1989)

- Sensory issues relating to autism (Bogdashina, 2003)

coupled with an awareness of:

- Behaviour support (LaVigna and Donnellan, 1986)

- Functional analysis.

This knowledge and understanding should be regarded as a critical resource as vital to successful intervention as any environmental change, physical intervention or piece of equipment.

Practical experience

Organisations recruiting staff teams to support individuals with autism and challenging behaviour are unlikely to consistently attract people who are endowed with a wealth of practical experience in this field. Such people are a rare commodity and organisations need to work hard to recruit and retain such people. Organisations invariably need to employ people who have a 'parallel' experience in the education or care services or who have made a concerted effort to gain experience in the field through voluntary or agency and supply work.

However, there are people who have accumulated vast experience in this area, often through many years of dedicated service. These people can form the nucleus of staff teams, passing the benefits of their experience on to others and thereby establishing a broad knowledge base within organisations and across the sector. Consequently, experienced practitioners offer two vital qualities to organisations – namely:

(a)   Skilful, practical, high quality support for individuals.

(b)   Role models for less experienced colleagues.

However, for many organisations, a significant proportion of their staff team will be relatively inexperienced. This is unavoidable and should prompt managers and leaders within those organisations to ensure that robust programmes of continuous training are consistently available. The people who receive this input become the next generation of experienced practitioners, the core of practitioners around whom organisations are formed.

People supporting individuals with autism and challenging behaviour are better able to support those individuals if they have experienced:

- over three years in general education or care services

- over two years in a specialised resource for individuals with challenging behaviour

- over two years in a specialised resource for individuals with autism

- effective professional development

- supportive networks of practice.

As a general rule, the more complex an individual, the greater the need for practical skill and pragmatic approaches. Alone, time served in this field is not enough; coupled with a good theoretical grounding and the 'right' personal and physical characteristics, practical experience is invaluable.

The following Skills and Understanding Matrix (Table 4.1) is intended to provide people supporting individuals with autism and challenging behaviour with a structured method for identifying their areas of strengths and areas which require further development. Crucially, this matrix provides a focus for further training or personal development and may enhance the quality of support which can be offered.

In order to complete this matrix people supporting individuals with autism and challenging behaviour should approach the exercise honestly, being neither too lenient nor too harsh in their self-evaluation. The closer the judgements are to reality, the greater the benefit to both the individual with autism and challenging behaviour and the person supporting them.

A single point should be allocated to each attribute it is judged a person has. Therefore, a maximum of 12 marks for personal characteristics, 5 marks for physical attributes, 7 marks for theoretical understanding and 5 marks for practical experience can be obtained. This gives an overall total of 29 marks against which people supporting individuals with autism and challenging behaviour can judge their capacity to perform effectively. Those attributes which do not attract a score can become priority areas for personal development.

Developing organisations

Supporting individuals with autism and challenging behaviour requires high quality teamwork and consistent collaboration. It is too demanding a role for any single person to effectively fulfil and whether the context is a family home, a school, a work-place environment, a college placement or a specialist residential setting, people supporting individuals with autism and challenging behaviour will themselves require continuous support. In developing organisations and, in this respect, we can consider the family unit an 'organisation', it is important to ensure that the people who comprise that organisation are able to become as effective as possible. (While it might seem an alien concept, families might benefit from thinking of themselves as an organisation when focusing on the challenges they face due to a family member's autism. It is important to maintain as normal a family life as possible for most of the time, but there are occasions when it might be useful to think organisationally.) Individually, a person's effect will be limited and temporary; working together as an organised team, people can make a positive and enduring difference.

Strong and effective organisations share four inextricably linked characteristics – namely:

- Consistent good practice

- Training and professional development

- Pastoral care

- Inter-organisational collaboration.

These underpin everything which that organisation achieves. By focusing particularly on these four characteristics, organisations can improve practice in a structured and cohesive fashion.

Consistent good practice

Organisations which provide effective support for individuals with autism and challenging behaviour invariably provide high quality practice across all aspects of their work. Quality

Table 4.1 Skills and Understanding Matrix

Personal characteristics	Physical attributes	Theoretical understanding	Practical experience
Calmness	Healthy	The triad of impairment	3 yrs' general services
Confidence	Fit	Theory of mind	2 yrs' challenging behaviour
Conviction	Co-ordinated	Executive function	2 yrs' autism
Courage	Alesrt	Central coherence theory	Effective prof. development
Creativity	Robust	Sensory issues	Supportive networks
Determination		Behaviour support	
Empathy		Functional analysis	
Honesty			
Humility			
Initiative			
Resilience			
Sympathy			
Total	Total	Total	Total

Overall score: ....

Key priorities for development

1.
2.
3.

 Positive Behaviour Strategies to Support Children and Young People with Autism,
Paul Chapman Publishing © Martin Hanbury, 2007

promotes and sustains quality and once a high standard has been reached, good organisations work hard to maintain their reputation and their purpose for being in existence. Among those organisations which are recognised as good quality providers practice is consistent day by day and across all aspects of an individual's life. For an individual with autism and challenging behaviour, inconsistent good practice is as detrimental as poor practice. Good practice should be a continuous experience and not an episodic collection of events. The greater the challenges an individual experiences, the greater the need for consistency.

Securing consistent good practice requires organisations to be thorough and candid in their self-evaluation processes. These processes can help organisations to identify their strengths and build upon these by ensuring that good practice is disseminated across the whole organisation. Crucially, people can isolate those factors which have contributed to the strengths within their organisations and endeavour to replicate these factors throughout the whole organisation.

Equally, the process of self-evaluation can enable organisations to determine the causes of weakness within the quality of provision they offer. This should not be an exercise in self-recrimination, but rather a process through which gaps in provision are noted and plans for remedying this are formed.

Once effective self-evaluation has taken place and strengths and weaknesses have been identified and addressed, organisations can consider how they might develop further and therefore both sustain and extend the consistent good practice they display. This phase involves building the capacity of the organisation to meet the evolving needs of the individuals it serves. This capacity building might involve the procurement of physical resources, the recruitment of staff team members, alterations to the physical environment or engagement with specialist support services. Crucially, capacity building and the development of any organisation must account for the changing state of an individual's needs. Individuals with autism and challenging behaviour rarely display a static profile of needs, and developments around individuals must accommodate the changing profile of needs each individual presents.

Organisations may benefit by structuring their development around standards frameworks such as those developed by the British Institute of Learning Disabilities (www.bild.org.uk/03tqn.htm) or the National Autistic Society's Accreditation Programme (www.nas.org.uk). Seeking external reference points for the development of an organisation can prove an effective means of focusing staff groups onto a structured series of standards which are broadly recognised as important in the provision of good quality care for individuals with autism.

Training and professional development

It has been acknowledged that developing the skills and understanding of a person who supports individuals with autism and challenging behaviour is a prerequisite for success. This development needs to take place within an organisational context to ensure that there is consistency in approaches and coherence in the overall objectives governing an organisation's professional development planning.

Effective organisations are able to structure training and professional development according to the requirements of specific roles within the organisation and the long-term aims of the organisation in meeting the needs of individuals with autism and challenging behaviour. This structure can be envisaged as a series of concentric circles with each progressive circle representing an increasing level of expertise. Within this model all members of the organisation undertake **core**

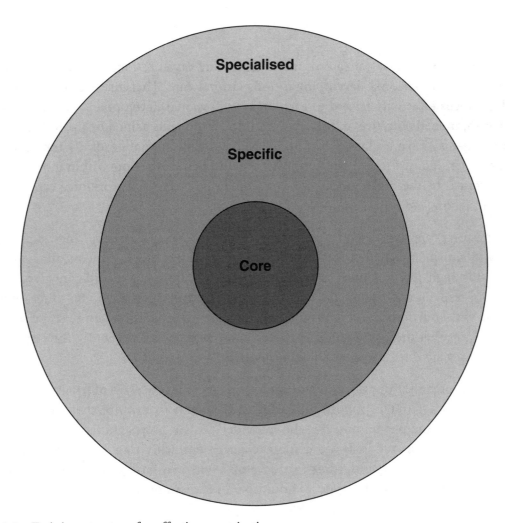

Figure 4.4   Training structure for effective organisations

training which is designed to equip people with the basic skills necessary to support individuals. Following this, the organisation might identify **specific** training for particular roles within the organisation. A third dimension of professional development might focus on highly **specialised** training aimed at developing expertise within the organisation which is proficient in delivering training within the organisation and externally. This structure is shown in Figure 4.4.

Organisations need to consider two key principles when developing their professional development programmes. First, there is a 'critical mass' of people at each dimension of training who need to have received a full package of that training. This figure will vary according to the size of the organisation. However, if there are insufficient numbers of people within a level who have been fully trained, then expertise becomes diluted and practice suffers accordingly.

Secondly, there are certain key strategic members within organisations who are best able to exemplify and disseminate good practice. Identifying these critical people enables organisations to ensure that training and professional development becomes embedded within the organisation. It is important to recognise that these people are not necessarily senior members of the organisation. Often these key players might be popular and well-respected members of the team, people with specific responsibility for areas of practice or key workers to particularly challenging individuals.

Pastoral care

When considering the pastoral care of members of any organisation, a distinction should be drawn between professional development and pastoral care. This distinction can be formed around the focus of activity related to each area. Professional development concerns attention to the developmental objectives of the organisation. The benefits gained by the individual member of the organisation are a by-product of the overall organisational needs. Pastoral care, on the other hand, is primarily focused on supporting the well-being of people within the organisation. Benefits accrued by the organisation as a consequence of increased workforce capability are a fortunate outcome and not the purpose of pastoral care.

Effective pastoral care is an essential component of any good organisation which supports individuals with autism and challenging behaviour. Living with, caring for or educating an individual with this high level of need is extremely stressful. Typically, people involved in these activities are resilient and optimistic; but there may be times when anybody, either living with or working with individuals with autism and challenging behaviour, might become susceptible to the pressures that they experience. However, these people are frequently the last people to realise this; they are often too busy coping to notice.

Consequently, organisations need to build into their regular processes of supervision and professional support, frequent opportunities for each person to explore their needs in a way which focuses on the person and not the 'provider'. This requires skilled input from others within the staff team and may necessitate engagement with established well-being programmes. Alternatively, organisations can develop their own 'in-house' systems for support. Whichever means is adopted, support should be a process and not an event and should be characteristically

- Individualised

- Person centred

- Confidential

- Consistent.

In supporting individuals with autism and challenging behaviour, it should be remembered that each person involved in the process has fundamental rights which must be observed. This includes that very special group of people who provide the support.

Inter-organisational collaboration

A final important element in developing ourselves consists of identifying those aspects of our practice which foster strong inter-organisational collaboration. Individuals with autism and challenging behaviour invariably receive services from a number of differing agencies. At the simplest level, this might involve the individual's family and their school or the family and social service departments. At more complex levels, an individual's needs may be served by their family, residential settings, schools, social services, voluntary organisations and specialist disciplines such as speech and language therapy or occupational therapy. Whatever the situation, it is vital that the consistency that is sought within organisations is secured across all aspects of an individual's life.

A critical development towards achieving this consistency has been the development of **person-centred planning** as an approach towards providing holistic support for individuals with disability (www.personcenteredplanning.org). This project can be extended into the lives of individuals with autism and challenging behaviour and where effective person-centred planning has occurred, there has been a directly related enhancement in the quality of life for individuals.

Alongside this approach, organisations can significantly enhance their practice by ensuring that they are aligned with one another in terms of ethos and practice. This is best achieved proactively – that is, not waiting until difficulties have occurred but rather collaborating across all aspects of an individual's life from the beginning of the relationship with other organisations. Collaboration can be focused in a number of areas including:

- Individual specific planning in order to develop practice together.

- Training together in order to secure shared understandings of approaches.

- Professional visits to one another's bases in order to share practice.

- Sharing employment of key staff members between organisations.

The better the quality of collaboration between organisations, the better the outcomes for the individual those organisations are supporting. Consequently, there is an obligation on each organisation working with an individual with autism and challenging behaviour to be outward looking and to seek to build strong links with others.

Key points

- People who support individuals with autism and challenging behaviour are part of a dynamic relationship.
- People who support individuals need to examine the ethics, reasons and aspirations which motivate them.
- Every person displays challenging behaviour at some time.
- There are identifiable qualities which characterise people who provide effective behaviour support. These can be grouped into four categories:
  (a) Personal characteristics
  (b) Physical attributes
  (c) Theoretical understanding
  (d) Practical experience.
- People supporting individuals need organisational support.
- People supporting individuals need to be self-analytical and able to identify their strengths and developmental needs.
- Organisations providing effective behaviour support are typically learning organisations.

CHAPTER 5

Developing the Learning Environment

This chapter includes:

- an examination of the term 'learning environment'
- an evaluation of safe, healthy and calm learning environments
- an assessment of relevant and motivating learning.

The learning environment

It is broadly recognised that a great deal of productive learning takes place well away from the classroom. This chapter will present the 'learning environment' as any setting in which people supporting individuals with autism and challenging behaviour are endeavouring to structure experiences and activities in order to support the progress of the individual they are supporting. This might involve environments such as schools, colleges, local shopping centres, family homes, local swimming pools, parks and many more settings which play an integral part in the life of an individual. Essentially, the learning environment is any setting which an individual encounters and through which they learn about the world around them.

In Chapter 2 we referred to LaVigna and Donnellan's (1986) consideration of the context within which behaviour occurs, noting that behaviour is profoundly influenced by the environment around a person. Learning is fundamentally 'a behaviour'; it is therefore contingent upon the context within which it occurs and reflective of that context. From this position it is a logical step to conclude that the 'learning environment' is a critical component in the life of a person with autism and challenging behaviour. If the learning environment can be successfully developed, the prospects for that individual are significantly enhanced.

Of all the elements which might affect an individual with autism and challenging behaviour, the learning environment is the variable which can most easily be influenced. We cannot readily alter a person's neurology or psychology; we cannot change their history, nor can we determine their future. We can, however, ensure that we create an optimum environment for learning via sound multi-agency collaboration, thorough planning and the procurement of sufficient resources. Consequently, there is an obligation to ensure that the environments that are created around an individual with autism and challenging behaviour represent the best efforts which people supporting that individual are able to make.

The primary objective should be to create an environment which is 'optimally stimulating' (Jordan and Powell, 1995) – that is, an environment which does not over-excite, intimidate or overload an individual with autism and yet is not stark, soulless and institutional. This is a difficult balance to achieve as the 'optimal' conditions may vary from day to day for an individual with autism according to a range of different variables. Invariably, the individual will share the living or working environment with other people, some of whom may themselves have autism and challenging behaviour. The needs of these other people, whether they be family members, colleagues, classmates or service users, may not be compatible with the conditions which have been identified as optimal. Consequently, people supporting individuals with autism and challenging behaviour are presented with a series of dilemmas which need to be addressed.

This process needs to begin with a simple, fundamental question, which is:

Is there a **primacy** of needs?

This means examining whether the degree of difficulty presented by the challenging behaviour an individual displays is such that all other considerations are put aside. In this case, the day-to-day variations which occur are reduced, leading to the development of a simple and secure environment. The needs of other people sharing that environment become secondary.

Where this cannot be reasonably and ethically agreed, an alternative environment needs to be found for either the person whose needs are primary or the other people who might share that environment. This is always an emotionally difficult conclusion to reach; it is sometimes the right thing to do.

If a decision is reached, that there is no primacy of needs and that the needs of every person sharing the environment can be accommodated, then people supporting the individual with autism and challenging behaviour should identify the following factors:

- The conditions which are **mutually beneficial**.

- The factors which create **stability** around these conditions.

- The **resources** that are required to maintain this stability.

Having established these factors, a 'best fit' for optimal conditions can be evolved around the needs of the individual and the others who share the environment.

As has been previously noted, optimum learning conditions are achieved by developing environments which are:

- safe

- healthy

- calm

and within which the learning provided is

- relevant

- motivating.

Securing these basic prerequisites is essential before any productive and positive learning can occur.

A safe learning environment

In creating the conditions in which an individual is best able to learn, the first consideration any person supporting that individual must make is whether or not the environment is safe. This process involves an honest and open appraisal of the conditions in which learning takes place and needs to account for both the **physical** environment of the learning context and the **social** environment within that learning context.

When evaluating the physical environment, seven critical factors need to be considered:

1 **Maintenance** – Is the fabric of the environment well maintained? A well-maintained environment shows respect for the dignity of the people living and working within that setting.

2 **Space** – Is there sufficient space in the environment to allow individuals' personal space to be respected? Remember a person with autism may well have a different experience of personal space from most other people.

3 **Clarity** – Is the purpose and function of the environment clear to individuals who live or work in it? Clarity avoids confusion; clutter causes chaos – clearly defined areas which contain only the materials that are necessary promote positive learning experiences.

4 **Decoration** – Is the setting decorated in a way which takes account of the sensory needs of individuals using the setting? The use of colour, the impact of natural light, the texture of carpets and furnishing are all important factors.

5 **Adaptation** – Is the environment adapted to fully meet the needs of the individuals within it? For some people with autism and challenging behaviour, special adaptations need to be made to the physical environment which might include developing safe areas or creating sound-proofed rooms.

6 **Accessibility** – Is the environment designed so that amenities such as arrival and departure points, toilets, bathrooms, dining areas and play areas are well located? Transitions are frequently a source of difficulty for people with autism – this needs to be considered when designing the physical environment.

7 **Leisure** – Is there a range of leisure opportunities available for individuals? The environment should promote choices for individuals by providing a number of different opportunities for relaxation and enjoyment.

Having considered these factors, the following guidance might prove helpful:

1 **Maintenance** – Ensure that the physical environment is checked regularly and frequently by a designated person or team. Identify those items within the environment which need to be checked on

   (a) a daily basis

   (b) a weekly basis

   (c) a monthly basis

   and create a simple and clear recording system to ensure that the checks have been carried out. Emphasise to everyone supporting the individual with autism and challenging behaviour that responsibility for the physical environment rests with every member of the team.

2 **Space** – Closely observe the personal space required by each individual you are supporting. Discuss the issues with a range of people, noting those times when individuals seem to distance themselves from others and the strategies individuals have evolved in order to secure their own personal space. Creating spaces within spaces can be very helpful so investigate whether small indoor tents might be helpful or whether furniture can be arranged to enable individuals to create 'bolt holes' for themselves.

3 **Clarity** – Ensure that the spaces around the individual you are supporting are always tidy and items are neatly arranged in boxes or placed on shelves or in cupboards. Use office dividers or other forms of screening to create areas for discrete activities. Alternatively use different coloured carpet tiles or sticking tape to define the purpose of an area within a room.

4 **Decoration** – There is clear evidence that individuals with autism are profoundly affected by the colours around them and the textures of materials close to them. While this will vary, there are general rules of thumb around adopting colours such as light blues or gentle aquamarines and sea greens to create a calm ambience. Similarly, it is wise to avoid harsh and abrasive materials, opting instead for soft, natural fibres.

5 **Adaptation** – There are very few purpose-built environments for individuals with autism and challenging behaviour and consequently adaptation is invariably a necessity. A comprehensive health and safety assessment of the environment needs to be conducted before any adaptation is made; it may be helpful to bring in a specialist health and safety adviser to support this as they will offer expertise and a neutral view. Use this baseline evaluation to adapt the environment to meet the individual's needs, focusing on a bespoke response to the specific challenges the individual presents.

6 **Accessibility** – Wherever possible individuals should have discrete access to the learning space they use without having to cross general or shared areas. Where transitions are problematic, they should be reduced to a bare minimum. If necessary, mealtimes

can be addressed within a learning space. Similarly, bathrooms and toilets can be located within discrete units.

7   **Leisure** – Ensure that individuals have easy access to their favourite pastimes and activities. Create a specific space within the learning environment for relaxation and leisure. Try and broaden the range of leisure activities an individual experiences by gradually introducing new ideas and experiences within these discrete spaces.

Arguably, the most important factors in any learning environment are the people who share that environment. Learning is about relationships and a learning environment is characterised by positive and respectful relationships. The social environment reflects the quality of these relationships and profoundly affects the learning which occurs in any setting. When evaluating the social environment, the following factors should be considered:

- **Belonging** – Is the social environment warm and friendly? Each individual should feel welcome at all times in the setting.

- **Valued** – Does every person in the setting feel valued? Praise, encouragement, celebration and affection should permeate all interactions at all times.

- **Repair** – How effectively are relationships repaired following difficult incidents? Individuals should be supported in restoring relationships while family or staff team members need access to support following difficult incidents.

- **Advocacy** – Do the individuals within the setting have a 'voice' which has a meaningful impact on the setting? Families and practitioners may need to be very creative in the ways in which they promote advocacy in their settings.

Accounting for these basic principles in evaluating the physical and social environment provides a firm foundation for developing a safe learning environment. From this foundation, people supporting individuals with autism and challenging behaviour need to engage in the process of **risk assessment**. It is important to understand risk assessment as a dynamic, interactive process which is continuously evolving to meet the changing needs of individuals and the changing conditions surrounding the individual. Risk assessment must be informed by observation, discussion and theoretical understanding and requires a collaborative approach to the analysis of hazards. Managing the risks that individuals and the people who support them face is a finely balanced and infinitely complex exercise in which accurate and continuous assessment is a critical tool.

Good risk assessment is extremely sensitive to the context which it serves. Consequently, it is neither appropriate to propose a universal format for risk assessment nor suggest a common procedure. However, there are certain basic principles which can be observed – namely:

- Know the individual.

- Identify the risks individuals present to themselves.

- Identify the risks individuals present to others.

- Identify the risks individuals present to the environment.

- Identify management strategies for each recognised risk.

- Evaluate the impact of these strategies on the degree of risk.

- Review the risk assessment on a regular and frequent basis.

Some organisations use these principles to develop scoring systems around risk and will designate a given level above which certain activities may not take place. Other organisations adopt a 'narrative' approach in which descriptions of risk are analysed and senior managers make decisions based on this. Examples of this are shown in Tables 5.2 and 5.3. These are not presented as exemplars of practice, but rather as examples of how the principles outlined above have been incorporated into practice.

In Tables 5.2 and 5.3 the term **'hazard'** represents the occurrence which causes danger to a person's health or safety. In rating this hazard, consideration should be given to the severity of injury which might be caused by this hazard on a scale of 1–10 in which 1 represents a minor injury such as a graze or small skin blemish and 10 represents a severe injury which endangers a person's life such as a heavy blow to the head or asphyxiation.

The terms **'management'** and **'control measures'** refer to the strategies which are implemented in order to reduce the danger presented by the hazard. Effective management of risk reduces the danger presented by hazards and therefore produces a lowered score relating to that hazard. It is important to note that while effective management reduces risk, it cannot eradicate it and the score related to the hazard may still exceed an acceptable level of risk.

Table 5.1 is intended to give some guidance on the rating of hazards. Each number on the scale is set alongside an example of the harm or damage which may occur as a consequence of an identified hazard.

People supporting individuals with autism and challenging behaviour might use this rating scale in evaluating the risk an individual presents to themselves, other people around them or the

Table 5.1   Rating scale

Rating	Harm to people	Damage to property
1	Reddened skin, discomfort	Walls or tables scribbled on
2	Marked skin, slight bruising	Books ripped
3	Minor abrasion, bruising	Furniture pushed over
4	Scratches, muscular pain	Objects thrown and broken
5	Bruising, bite marks	Faeces smeared
6	Broken skin, muscular strain	Doors kicked and indented
7	Bleeding, ligament damage	Windows smashed
8	Deep wounds, limb incapacitated	Walls punctured
9	Severe blood loss, bone fracture	Flooding
10	Blindness, brain damage	Arson

Table 5.2   Risk Assessment – Scoring System

Name:	D.o.B.	Context:
Medical Needs:	Communication:	Likes/Dislikes:

Hazard	*Risk to self*	Management		Rating		Score

Hazard	*Risk to others*	Management		Rating		Score

Hazard	*Risk to the environment*	Management		Rating		Score

| | | | | | Total | |

Does this total exceed the agreed amount for risk assessment?   yes   no

If this level of risk exceeds the agreed level, what measures need to be introduced to further control the risk?

1.
2.

To be reviewed:	Signed:	Date:

Positive Behaviour Strategies to Support Children and Young People with Autism,
Paul Chapman Publishing © Martin Hanbury, 2007

Table 5.3   Risk Assessment – Descriptions of Risk

Key: H = High, M = Medium, L = Low   A = Acceptable, U = Unacceptable

Name:		D.o.B.:		Context:
Medical Needs:		Communication:		Likes/Dislikes:

Hazard	Impact	Prob.	Control measures	Risk
Self	H M L	H M L		A U
	H M L	H M L		A U
	H M L	H M L		A U
Others	H M L	H M L		A U
	H M L	H M L		A U
	H M L	H M L		A U
Enviromental	H M L	H M L		A U
	H M L	H M L		A U
	H M L	H M L		A U

Do the control measures implemented reduce the risk presented by these hazards to an acceptable degree?	yes	no

If this level of risk exceeds the agreed level, what measures need to be introduced to further control the risk?

1.

2.

To be reviewed:	Signed:	Date:

Positive Behaviour Strategies to Support Children and Young people with Autism,
Paul Chapman Publishing © Martin Hanbury, 2007

physical environment. Try and relate the actions of the individual you are supporting, or their equivalence, to the examples given. From this, attach a score to the risk presented and use this to consider the scale of the risk this individual presents.

Risk assessments need to take account of the perspective of the individual who is being supported. It is vital that both the physical and the social setting are viewed from the standpoint of a person with autism. This is essential for two key reasons – namely:

1   Many people with autism have a very limited sense of danger and whilst an environment might appear safe, there may be aspects of that environment which present dangers to a particular individual.

2   Many people with autism develop a number of apparently irrational fears around issues which are unlikely to endanger them. Consequently, environments which might appear secure and comfortable to most people may cause anxiety for the individual with autism.

Therefore, consideration must be given to those 'real risks' which emerge due to the impulsive and often unpredictable nature of people with autism and to those 'perceived dangers' which a person with autism experiences.

It is important for people supporting individuals with autism and challenging behaviour to develop a broad understanding of a safe learning environment. The process of securing a safe learning environment involves not only the basic requirements of any health and safety assessment but also the development of an environment which seeks to promote positive behaviour. Attention to safety in this sense is not simply a reactive response to hazards within the environment. It is a holistic and proactive approach through which individuals are supported by the physical and social environment around them thereby reducing the number of potential hazards within the environment.

A healthy learning environment

A healthy learning environment has many different elements and it is important that each of these is engaged when determining how healthy a learning environment is. When considering how healthy a learning environment is, people supporting individuals with autism and challenging behaviour need to address the following key issues:

- Nutrition

- Medication

- Cleanliness

- Exercise

- Mental health.

Any person's well-being is ultimately dependent upon their diet in terms of both its content and its regulation. This is no less true of individuals with autism than it is of anyone else. However, the issue of diet and autism has been so widely researched and reported in recent years that it has generated an overwhelming mass of literature which for many people is both contentious and confusing.

There are strong bodies of opinion which maintain that many people with autism benefit from restricted diets, particularly diets that are gluten and casein free. Alongside these ideas other theories related to enzyme or vitamin deficiency are prevalent and there is a gathering body of scientific evidence to give all of these ideas some credence. (For more detailed information on Autism and Diet visit www.nas.org.uk as a starting point for recommended reading in this area.)

A further major consideration related to issues of autism and diet relates to the extremes of hyper- and hypo-sensitivity which many people with autism experience. Naturally, if the sensations of taste and smell are affected, people with autism are likely to find many foods aversive and therefore develop very restricted dietary regimes. Similarly people with autism might develop a preference for strange combinations of foods or irregular times for eating and drinking. There may be sound reasons for discouraging individuals from diets of this nature but there is an equally compelling rationale related to that individual's right to determine their favourite foods and their rights to access food and drink.

These various factors have a profound effect on the nutrition of people with autism. While there are clear and well-understood ideas of what a healthy diet might be, achieving these ideals is not necessarily straightforward. People supporting individuals with autism and challenging behaviour need to balance these competing elements when developing a healthy and enjoyable diet.

It may be necessary at times to accept the diet the individual chooses simply because it represents nutrition of some sort. It then becomes necessary to supplement the individual's diet while introducing a series of proactive programmes aimed at increasing the range and flexibility of the individual's diet. This is best achieved incrementally and may involve strategies focused on increasing an individual's tolerance of the 'presence' of a range of foods rather than inviting the individual to taste or smell them. When the presence of the food is no longer aversive, there is a greater probability that the individual will try it for themselves.

Many individuals with autism and challenging behaviour take medication on a regular basis. Sometimes this medication is prescribed to ameliorate the challenges the individual presents. Other individuals may take medication for epilepsy or other identifiable conditions while almost all individuals will need medication at some point in their lives in order to address the same medical needs anybody is likely to encounter.

Apart from the last example, the medication administered to individuals with autism and challenging behaviour is invariably powerful. Naturally, this has a profound effect on the individual's well-being and a continuous process of review should be in place for all individuals taking medication of this nature. Despite these precautions, there are times when medication can provide an important opportunity for developing programmes of learning for an individual which reduce the degree of challenging behaviour the individual presents thereby lessening the need for medication.

Most people recognise the need for cleanliness in any learning environment. When supporting individuals with autism and challenging behaviour this need is particularly pronounced due to a number of factors associated with the condition. First, the risk of contamination due to increased incidents of injury needs to be carefully managed. Any injury which breaks the skin leaves the body open to infection and therefore demands that all possible measures are taken to ensure that the environment is clean.

Secondly, many individuals with autism and challenging behaviour have significant learning disabilities and severe developmental delay. This produces a number of difficulties for people supporting these individuals in terms of creating a clean and healthy environment. Individuals with any marked developmental delay may well be incontinent and therefore require substantial support in remaining clean and comfortable. Failure to do this creates a risk of infection and jeopardises not only an individual's health but also their dignity. In addition to this, many people with severe developmental delays may well explore items using their mouths, making them prone to infection from unhygienic conditions. Related to this is a condition known as **pica** which a proportion of people with autism and challenging behaviour display. Individuals with pica have a tendency to ingest inappropriate materials which therefore leaves them prone to both infection and poisoning. Consequently, clean learning environments reduce the risk of contamination for these individuals.

Exercise is a crucial part of learning for any individual with autism and challenging behaviour. A good regime of exercise not only enhances an individual's physical health but contributes significantly to their well-being generally. A regular, well-structured daily routine of exercise is imperative for all individuals with autism and challenging behaviour. This daily fitness plan provides structure to the individual's daily routine, promotes an individual's health, 'burns off' excess energy, provides opportunities for success and enhanced self-esteem and encourages co-operation among peers and between individuals and those supporting them.

However, despite the unquestionable benefits of exercise for individuals with autism and challenging behaviour, there are a number of difficulties which must be overcome before the routine can be established. These obstacles include:

- Sensory difficulties

- Resistance to change

- Effect of medication

- Over-stimulation.

Sensory difficulties can inhibit an individual's capacity to engage in exercise if they are not addressed effectively. Individuals who find physical contact aversive may not be able to tolerate being moved by another person into a required position and yet may not be able to process language sufficiently well in order to follow instructions. For these individuals the use of clear and simple visual demonstration may provide a solution. Many people with autism learn particularly well from videos and DVDs which build on the characteristic visual strengths of learners with autism. The range of exercise videos and DVDs available offer a possible solution to this problem.

Other sensory difficulties may emerge due to the places that exercise typically takes place such as large sports halls or swimming baths. These locations tend to be acoustically very challenging to people with auditory sensitivities and it may be more productive to consider alternative and more familiar venues for exercise routines.

Consideration should also be given to the physical sensations which are experienced during exercise which might be frightening to an individual who may not fully comprehend what is happening to their body. The increases in heart rate, temperature and adrenalin which are pleasurable for most people may threaten individuals who do not understand what is happening and may not be aware that the effect is temporary. It might be helpful to consider ways in which exercise routines can be graduated so that there are no sudden or unpredictable upsurges in the physiological effects experienced by individuals.

Resistance to change remains a defining feature of autism and entails that any new learning needs to be creatively and carefully planned. Introducing an exercise routine into anyone's lifestyle is difficult and is even more so when an individual may not be able to fully appreciate the benefits available. People supporting individuals with autism and challenging behaviour should introduce exercise routines according to the same sound principles which characterise effective learning programmes for people with autism across all fields. Therefore, exercise routines should be introduced:

1   Individually – Tailor each element of the routine to individual needs.

2   Incrementally – Introduce each part of the programme gradually.

3   Visually – Ensure instructions are provided in clear, permanent visual forms.

4   Consistently – Repetition and predictability are prerequisites for success.

5   Sympathetically – Be aware of the experience from the perspective of the individuals.

6   Positively – Encourage and praise all efforts.

A significant proportion of individuals with autism and challenging behaviour are prescribed a range of strong medications which have a profound effect on their perception of and relationship with the world around them. When implementing exercise routines, thought should be given to the effects of this medication. Individuals may be tired or sluggish due to the effect of medication. Their balance and co-ordination may be affected while their proprioception (their capacity for understanding their position and location in physical space) may be significantly disrupted by medication. People supporting individuals may consider whether there are optimum times of the day for exercise or whether individuals benefit from shorter, more frequent episodes of exercise.

Many individuals with autism and challenging behaviour find regulating their behaviour difficult. The excitement and enjoyment that accompanies exercise for many people can create problems for individuals who may not be able to achieve a calm and steady state following the end of the exercise session or who become too stimulated by the heightened levels of arousal required for exercise. It may be necessary to integrate exercise with relaxation sessions thereby managing the amount of adrenalin produced by exercise. Relaxation sessions may be introduced at the beginning or end of sessions or interspersed with periods of activity throughout the whole session. Once again, understanding the needs of the individual is of paramount importance in planning these sessions.

The final component of a healthy learning environment relates to an individual's mental health. This is an aspect of an individual's health that is sometimes overlooked in the field of autism and challenging behaviour because of the complexity of the condition and the difficulty health-care professionals encounter in establishing meaningful and consistent criteria for diagnosis. However, it must be recognised that an individual with autism and challenging behaviour is as likely to experience mental health problems as any other person. In fact, it is arguable that these individuals are more likely to experience such problems given the fact that they are often anxious, frustrated, isolated, confused and experience low self-esteem.

The treatment of mental health problems requires skilled, professional care and should not be addressed by anyone other than specialists in the field. However, people supporting individuals with autism and challenging behaviour need to be open to the possibility of mental health issues significantly impacting on the lives of the individuals they support and alert to indicators of these issues.

A calm learning environment

Chapter 3 focused on the importance of achieving optimum conditions for learning by identifying periods of calm in an individual's daily routine. A critical factor in establishing and maintaining calmness involves manipulating the environment around the individual so that it supports productive and positive behaviour patterns. As has previously been discussed, it is vital to analyse the environment from the perspective of the individual who is being supported. Elements of the environment that might promote calm for most people might not for a person with autism. For example, aromatherapy may be a calming experience for some people but aversive or over-stimulating for a person with heightened olfactory sensitivities. Equally, certain types of music may calm the majority of people but have unpleasant connotations for the individual who is being supported. There are no 'off-the-peg solutions'; nothing can be assumed.

However, there are a number of principles based upon established practice which are recognised as supporting the development of a calm learning environment. First, the learning environment needs to be a **'low arousal'** environment. This idea relates to the notion of optimal stimulation and is proposed because for the vast majority of individuals with autism and challenging behaviour exciting or 'arousing' environments do not represent the optimum stimulus. Consequently, while it is important to avoid Spartan and institutionalised environments, it is equally important to ensure that the environment does not overburden the individual who is supported in that environment.

Secondly, it must be recognised that the routines and practices within an environment are an integral part of that environment. Consequently, these features of the environment should be as structured as the physical fabric of the environment. In order to promote this, routines and practices should become as **predictable** as possible, enabling the individual supported within that environment to develop a coherent understanding of the whole environment. Naturally there are arguments about developing heavily routinised environments including the fact that the 'real world' is unpredictable and that predictability can undermine spontaneous activity.

However, it must be recognised that individuals with autism and challenging behaviour may not be able to cope with a more 'realistic' or spontaneous experience. After all, an individual's response to naturalistic settings in the past has been the reason that the individual is now considered 'challenging'. It is important to plan ahead to a time when more realistic and spontaneous elements can be incrementally introduced into the life of the individual being supported. However, during the development of the learning environment, a conservative and cautious approach is more likely to provide the stability which will be the bedrock of future progress.

Related to this feature of the environment is the need to secure **consistency**. It is reasonable to estimate that an individual with autism and challenging behaviour receiving 24 hour support will work with at least a dozen people a week. In some cases it will be many more. This arises because individuals with autism and challenging behaviour invariably require high levels of staffing in order to provide adequate support.

Yet, it is generally acknowledged that individuals with autism encounter difficulties in forming relationships and adapting to change. Therefore this aspect of the support offered to individuals with autism and challenging behaviour presents a central conundrum in that there needs to be a large team supporting the individual yet the individual may not easily cope with the numbers of people involved.

In order to minimise the difficulties which arise from this conundrum, organisations need to consider two inter-related elements of consistency – namely:

1   Consistency in practice.

2   Consistency in personnel.

Achieving consistency in one of these elements tends to promote consistency across the other. For example, consistency in practice leads to success which encourages and motivates the staff team. This enhances an organisation's capacity to retain members of staff and therefore reduces the turnover of staff which in turn leads to greater consistency in practice. This virtuous circle is the basis for successful intervention for individuals with autism and challenging behaviour. Investing in consistency is a worthwhile and productive investment of time and energy (see 'Developing Organisations' in Chapter 4).

The final element to be considered when developing a calm learning environment is the need to provide suitable **relaxation and recreation** opportunities. Everybody has a need for 'time out' and this is perhaps even more important for individuals with autism and challenging behaviour given the stresses and pressures which they experience for much of the time.

Typically, individuals with autism and challenging behaviour display a narrow range of inter-ests or leisure pursuits and consequently identifying activities which are productive is prob-lematic. However, it is not necessary to provide a broad and rich menu of possibilities but rather to focus on what the individual is known to enjoy and then, over time, to try and broaden this.

Naturally the need for relaxation and recreation needs to be incorporated into planning an envi-ronment which is 'low arousal', predictable and consistent. Table 5.4 may help in this process. This table is intended to be used as a tool to enable people to reflect on whether a learning envi-ronment is likely to be calm. It simply asks people supporting individuals with autism and chal-lenging behaviour if the critical elements for promoting a calm environment are in place. In completing this table, it is important to adopt the perspective of the individual with autism and challenging behaviour, noting what may or may not be stimulating, predictable or relaxing from their point of view.

Table 5.4   The Calm Environment Predictor

Arousal		Predictability		Consistency		Relaxation and recreation	
List those elements of the environment which are stimulating or distracting for the individual in the left-hand column. List the current control for each in the right-hand column.		List those aspects of the environment which are unpredictable to the individual in the left-hand column and those which are predictable in the right-hand column.		List each person involved in the individual's life each week in the left-hand column. Indicate which of these people has received core training in the right-hand column.		List the opportunities for relaxation and recreation available to the individual in the left-hand column. Indicate how much time per week the individual engages in each activity.	
Stimuli	Control	Unpredictable	Predictable	Name	Training	Activity	Time
Do you consider the learning environment to be 'low arousal'?		How predictable is the learning environment for the individual?		Is their consistency across practice and personnel?		Are there sufficient opportunities for the individual to relax and enjoy themselves?	

Positive Behaviour Strategies to Support Children and Young people with Autism,
Paul Chapman Publishing © Martin Hanbury, 2007

Relevant learning content

At the outset of this chapter the learning environment was described as any setting in which activities were structured in order to support the progress of individuals with autism and challenging behaviour. This includes home environments, school and pre-school settings, colleges, the local community and a host of other environments. What makes an environment a 'learning environment' is the learning it offers. Therefore a school is just a collection of buildings if there is no learning taking place, the local community a distant, abstract concept if an individual is not learning to function effectively within it.

Critical to the quality of learning is the **relevance** of what is being learnt. This is true for all learners, at all levels and in all settings and for individuals with autism and challenging behaviour this is especially so. Individuals with autism and challenging behaviour invariably experience great difficulties in learning. Learning causes stress and demands a great deal from individuals. Therefore, if an individual is going to be faced with experiences which cause them anxiety and difficulty, there is a moral obligation to ensure that the learning is of direct value to that individual.

This requires people supporting individuals with autism and challenging behaviour to critically evaluate the learning objectives identified for individuals by asking:

1   Why has this objective been chosen?

2   How will this objective improve the quality of the individual's life?

3   Does the individual understand the purpose of this objective?

4   Who benefits from this objective?

5   Is this objective realistic?

If the answers to these questions are not entirely focused on the individual's needs, then the learning content cannot be considered relevant.

Relevant learning content should be:

■   oriented to the learner

■   set in an immediate time-frame

■   realistically achievable therefore promoting success

■   bespoke – tailored to individual needs and learning styles.

Before each learning session, people supporting individuals with autism and challenging behaviour should ask a simple question:

Why am I doing this?

Motivating learning content

Not only should learning content be relevant, but it should be **motivating**. The relevance of the learning content and its capacity for motivating the learner are allied but are not the same thing.

As a general rule, if something is meaningful for a person, they are more likely to be motivated to learn it, more likely to find intrinsic value in the work itself. However, it is possible for something to be important for an individual to learn but not particularly enjoyable for them to engage with. Therefore, it becomes important to develop ways of working which enable relevant learning content to be motivating for individuals. Invariably this depends on the way in which learning opportunities are presented.

If the learning is **accessible** to the individual in terms of its cognitive demands, it is more likely to remain motivating. Similarly if the learning is based around activities the individual enjoys, it is more likely to be of **interest** to the individual. Where learning content and the means through which it can be delivered are not intrinsically motivating for individuals, the use of **rewards** or associated **token systems** can be very effective. People supporting individuals with autism and challenging behaviour must be prepared to employ whatever means are necessary in order to provide learning opportunities, including the use of tangible rewards such as favourite toys, food and drinks. While there may be reasonable concerns about whether using rewards might create further difficulties, if a decision has been made that a learning objective is important, then the use of rewards is justified.

Key points

- Learning is a behaviour human beings are predisposed to.
- The learning environment is any setting through which a person learns about the world around them.
- Effective learning environments are
  - (a) Safe
  - (b) Healthy
  - (c) Calm.
- Effective learning content is
  - (a) Relevant
  - (b) Motivating.
- Risk assessment is a critical element in developing the learning environment.
- Controlling the stimuli within an environment is vital in promoting effective learning environments.
- Predictability and consistency from the perspective of an individual with autism support effective learning environments.

CHAPTER 6

Supporting Others

This chapter includes:

- an emphasis on working supportively and collaboratively
- a discussion of ways in which families can be supported
- a suggestion for Inset training.

Sharing knowledge, supporting others

There is no doubt that supporting individuals with autism and challenging behaviour is a complex and highly demanding endeavour. People who provide this support effectively are committed and skilled and are invariably part of a team of like-minded relatives or colleagues. There are increasing examples of good practice in the field of behaviour support and this is a testament to the effectiveness of skilled, proactive intervention and the quality of training and development opportunities available to people supporting individuals.

However, there remains a need to disseminate good practice further for a number of reasons. First, high quality support for individuals with autism and challenging behaviour is by no means comprehensive and universal. There are still situations in which individuals are not receiving the standard of care and education which should be theirs by right. Until this situation is rectified, people involved in this field should be striving to ensure that best practice is shared as broadly as possible.

Secondly, there is evidence of an **increasing prevalence** of autism. This does not necessarily mean that there will be an increase in the numbers of individuals with autism and challenging behaviour but it is a possibility which must be considered. If there is a related rise in the prevalence of individuals with autism and challenging behaviour, then there will be a demand for a greater number of people supporting these individuals. These people will need to be equipped with a high degree of skill and knowledge and this resource will come from within the field.

Alongside this factor, there is a changing social context which profoundly affects this area and will continue to do so over the forthcoming years. **Inclusion** has become a strong and enduring influence on practice across all sectors of care and education and is driving developments in the support that is provided for people with autism and challenging behaviour. On one level, there is recognition of the right of individuals to be socially included. This means supporting access to a range of social and communal activities, which places a unique set of demands on individuals and the people supporting them. At another level, schools and colleges are obliged to make every effort to include all learners and in some cases this will require the inclusion of individuals with autism and challenging behaviour. Consequently, there will be changes in curriculum and methodologies to accommodate the particular learning needs of this group.

Each of these reasons demands that the wealth of knowledge and understanding within the field of autism and challenging behaviour be shared among the increasing number of people who will be called on to support individuals. This sharing of knowledge, understanding and practice should be underpinned by several ethical principles – namely:

1   There is an obligation to share knowledge, understanding and practice among organisations supporting individuals with autism and challenging behaviour.

2   Organisations should critically evaluate the quality of the training and professional development opportunities they provide to their team members and to other external agents.

3   People supporting individuals with autism and challenging behaviour should continuously seek improvements in the quality of their understanding and practice. Improvements should be shared with others.

4   There should not be a hierarchy of expertise but rather an open exchange of ideas, experiences, problems and solutions.

5   Organisations should encourage constructive criticism and offer open and honest appraisals of one another's practice. The boundaries between agencies should be removed in order to provide a holistic approach to supporting individuals.

These principles are intended to work against the 'territorialism' and 'defensiveness' which is still evident in certain areas. Improving the quality of life for individuals with autism and challenging behaviour requires a holistic approach based on collaboration and honesty. Ultimately, this way is the only way.

Supporting families

In Chapter 4 it was suggested that families think of themselves as 'organisations' for the purposes of developing behaviour support strategies. This does not mean that the love, warmth, vitality and the singular preciousness of family life should be in any way reduced when supporting an individual with autism and challenging behaviour. The notion of 'families-as-organisations' is directed at the practical arrangements which need to be implemented in order to effectively support the individual with autism and challenging behaviour. Families need to identify the strengths they have as a group of people, the advantages their personal circumstances bring and the benefits the extended family and local community offer. Alongside this, families need to recognise the physical, emotional and financial limitations of what they can provide and identify and access support to compensate for this.

Like all organisations, families should be considering the ways in which they can collaborate with other organisations to provide a holistic approach to supporting the individual. These collaborations are reciprocal relationships which fall into one of two main categories – namely:

■ Family–family support

■ Family–practitioner support.

Each of these relationships has specific qualities which can be of great benefit to families. Families, as 'organisations', should consider how they can develop complementary packages of support derived from these two sources and how they may contribute to knowledge and understanding in their work with others.

Family–family support

The greatest source of understanding and advice for families supporting individuals with autism and challenging behaviour is other families in the same position. Other families offer unique insights derived from their shared experience of living with a child, brother, sister or grandchild who presents significant challenges to the family unit. Real understanding of the emotional complexity of this situation can only be claimed by others who live through the same experiences. Consequently, support among families is invaluable as difficulties, successes, problems and solutions are shared with other people whose understanding is grounded in personal experience.

However, the pressures of living with a family member with autism and challenging behaviour entail that many families become isolated and therefore unable to engage with other families. Consequently, the people who will benefit most from support and the people who are best equipped to provide that support find difficulty in meeting together because of the nature of the issues they require support for. This central paradox needs to be actively removed from the situation – that is, families and the practitioners who support them need to actively establish family-oriented support groups and provide the means by which these groups can be sustained.

The greatest obstacle facing families and the practitioners who support them in forming these groups relates to **child care**. The following options may be considered:

1 Obtain funding to arrange specialist child care facilities organised by practitioners experienced in the field while parent groups hold meetings.

2 Establish a child-minding circle enabling families to cover one another on a rota basis while other members of the group meet.

3 Organise 'away-days' enabling child care issues to be concentrated into a fixed time.

All of these options need to be thought through thoroughly with particular attention paid to child protection issues. Parents must be confident that the people they are leaving their children with are suitable and should seek advice from professional bodies such as their local Children and Young People's Services as to how these assurances can be secured.

If the obstacle of child care can be overcome, **family support networks** can be a rich source of information and advice. Organised around the particular concerns of participants, networks might want to adopt ideas from established groups and consider a programme of events including:

- Specialist workshops – Inviting speakers from the field of autism to give presentations to the families.

- Finance – Drawing on the experience of other families in obtaining benefits such as the Disability Living Allowance, Direct Payments, grants for modifications for the house or mobility allowances.

- Entitlements – Advice on their family member's legal entitlement in terms of education, respite care, access to community facilities or employment.

- Handy hints – Pooling 'top tips' on a broad range of issues from hair-brushing to bedtime routines to car seats and many more.

- Medical intervention – Sharing information on local healthcare practitioners who are 'autism friendly' such as GPs, dentists.

- Respite care – Discussion of the respite care available in the area and the necessary steps to be taken to improve this where it is considered inadequate.

- Holidays – Focusing on the most autism-friendly venues and destinations people have encountered.

- Siblings – Sharing concerns, ideas about the effect on siblings of a challenging child within the family; planning events specifically for the benefit of siblings (see www.nas.org.uk for further information on supporting siblings).

From this menu of possibilities, families can develop strong and supportive networks which combine practical advice and information with a unique understanding of the issues which families supporting individuals with autism and challenging behaviour face on a day-to-day basis.

Family–practitioner support

Without the wholehearted support of families, practitioners cannot hope to succeed in their practice with individuals with autism and challenging behaviour. Given the complex nature of individuals with autism and challenging behaviour, a range of different perspectives need to be understood before effective behaviour support strategies can be implemented. Families and practitioners need to share their understanding of the individual they are supporting in a reciprocal dialogue which is:

- Equal

- Open

- Honest

- Non-judgemental

- Continuous.

From this collaboration, a sound basis for the development of effective strategies can be established.

Practitioners are in a position to contribute to families' quality of life by providing a number of different elements to the processes of behaviour support. First, practitioners are able to offer an **external** perspective on the progress an individual is making. This perspective is not superior to the one families hold but it is different and may therefore offer insights which cannot be obtained from within the family unit.

Secondly, the infrastructure of professional organisations such as schools, residential facilities and employers enables them to access training and development opportunities which are not readily available to families. Consequently, an up-to-date generic understanding of autism and challenging behaviour may be developed within organisations more easily than it can within families. Therefore practitioners may be able to help inform understanding by disseminating the knowledge their work enables them to accumulate.

Arising from this, there is an onus on professional organisations to provide training opportunities to families via programmes such as conferences and **parent workshops**. These workshops can address a range of issues including:

- Understanding Autism

- Developing Communication Strategies

- Complementary Therapies

- Sensory Issues

- Play and Leisure Activities.

These workshops differ from the mutual support provided by family networks because they involve engaging with practitioners with a specialism in the particular topic they are addressing. This can offer insights and a degree of understanding which may not be accessible other than through this means.

Practitioners can also offer an informed understanding of the 'political landscape' which influences the lives of individuals. This can enable families to make decisions based around an awareness of local level developments within councils and, to some extent, national perspectives regarding legislation and government initiatives. The broader perspectives which can be offered by experienced practitioners can help families plan for the longer term and play an active role in shaping the future for the individual they support.

Practitioners are also in a position to guide families towards useful and up-to-date **research** which might be helpful in developing behaviour strategies. In some circumstances, families and practitioners may be in a position to conduct formal research and report this to a wider audience. There is a wealth of skill, understanding and commitment across the field of autism and challenging behaviour which lies with people at the 'front-line' of support. This expertise can be shared more broadly if families and practitioners are able to engage in the processes of research and reporting.

Supporting practitioners

Practitioners who support individuals with autism and challenging behaviour develop skills and understandings which are an invaluable resource. Sharing this expertise is critical for the improvement of the lives of individuals with autism and challenging behaviour. Throughout the exercise all parties should be regarded as learners; good learning affects everyone in the vicinity. However, there will be those whose understanding and knowledge is more developed in this field and who therefore can provide a broader range of insights to the difficulties which individuals with autism and challenging behaviour may encounter. Therefore the dissemination of skills and knowledge can take place on several levels depending on the relative understanding the participants in the exercise hold.

The processes through which practitioners support one another might be characterised as:

- Dialogue

- Cascade

- Network.

Dialogue is support between practitioners who share a similar level of expertise and specialist knowledge in the field of autism and challenging behaviour. Often this will be at a high level and will involve practitioners addressing difficulties at the cutting edge of the field either because they are particularly extreme or intractable problems, or because they represent innovations in improving the quality of life for individuals with autism and challenging behaviour.

Cascade is support that is offered between practitioners in which one partner in the process is significantly more experienced and knowledgeable than the other participant. This involves the more experienced partner passing on information, ideas and suggestions to the other partner in order to improve the other's understanding and practice. This is the most commonly used approach in professional development and incorporates Inset Days, specialist training and conferences.

Network is support offered by an eclectic group of providers and practitioners. It is a looser alliance of providers for individuals with autism and challenging behaviour and exists to offer 'moral' support as well as to share information and understanding. Network support derives its strength from its informality and the fact that it does not presuppose an agenda whereas both dialogue and cascade methods of support need to have a clear purpose and set of intended outcomes in order to be effective.

Each of these means of practitioner support has a specific purpose and a distinct series of principles which should guide activity. Practitioners engaged in dialogue should aim to:

- develop innovative practice

- share successes and frustrations

- combine to secure high quality training opportunities

- spend time in one another's settings

- compare the training and development opportunities they offer to other organisations.

Established, high quality specialist providers are in a position to move practice forward and to significantly improve the quality of life for individuals with autism and challenging behaviour. Historically, it has been experienced, committed practitioners with a well-developed knowledge and understanding of autism and challenging behaviour that have created new ways of approaching the difficulties faced in this field. At the current time, experienced and effective practitioners remain the most suitable people to innovate and contribute to our understanding of the field.

When experienced, established and effective practitioners work alongside colleagues who are relatively less knowledgeable about the field of autism and challenging behaviour, the nature of support alters. In this situation, one partner takes a lead role and identifies a 'curriculum' for the other partner. This cascade of knowledge and understanding is necessary in many circumstances, simply because there are not enough experienced practitioners to meet the needs of the increasing population of individuals with autism. Consequently, there is a pressing need to disseminate knowledge to meet the demands faced by organisations in addressing the needs of the individuals they support.

While this process of support is typically 'instructional' it can be interactive, stimulating and beneficial to both the 'teacher' and the 'taught'. The most effective sessions involve lively explorations of the key theoretical frameworks underpinning current understanding of autism and challenging behaviour and a consideration of the ethics and principles which guide practice. Practitioners either seeking or providing this type of support need to consider:

- the starting point of the practitioners receiving training

- the logistics of delivering training

- the resources required to deliver effective training

- the impact of training on the receiving organisation

- the impact of training on the supporting organisation.

Considering the prior knowledge of any learner is a basic requirement of any teaching process. Coupled with this is a need to understand people's learning styles. Naturally, the closer the relationship between 'trainer' and 'student', the more likely it is that an informed understanding of prior knowledge and learning style can be secured. However, the nature of training in this context is often such that the practitioner delivering training has little knowledge of these key elements in the learning process.

Therefore, practitioners providing training may survey the learning group prior to delivering training in order to determine general levels of:

- experience of autism

- experience of challenging behaviour

- theoretical understanding of autism and challenging behaviour

- previous relevant training

- the various roles within the organisation of members of the group

- the academic background of members of the group

- the outcomes the organisation wishes to achieve.

Determining this information will enable 'trainers' to refine a curriculum to the needs of the group. For example, a group which consists of largely inexperienced practitioners at an early stage in their understanding of autism and challenging behaviour generally benefits from a comparatively narrow content focus delivered in discrete elements across several sessions, preferably over a number of weeks. This allows people time to absorb information and reflect on its application to their particular circumstances.

Training methods should focus on establishing an understanding of the impact of the fundamental features of autism and the mechanisms which drive and maintain challenging behaviour. This can be achieved by describing and explaining theoretical models at a foundation level and then engaging participants in discussions about the effect these might have on an individual. Training at this level of understanding is most effective when it is broken into distinct areas of focus. Table 6.1 offers a programme for training which can be used in conjunction with the **training materials** provided in the Appendix to Chapter 6 which follows this chapter. These materials may be photocopied as handouts, transferred onto slides or used as a basis for slideshows according to the needs of the trainer.

People leading training sessions need to present a coherent and dedicated package of support for practitioners. This should be a structured programme delivered over a defined period of time, ideally within one month in order to enable people to form conceptual links and consolidate their learning. Trainers following the schedule presented below should use the materials as a basis for discussion and link these materials into the real-life experiences of the people they are training. Wherever possible, trainers should encourage people to identify links between the individual they work with and the theoretical concept being described.

Where practitioners form networks for support there needs to be an open and honest ethos which enables colleagues to discuss the concerns they encounter and the successes they have secured. This drawing together of practitioners involved in the same type of work without any judgements being made of performance or 'value for money' can provide unconditional support for colleagues and a fertile ground for the discussion of new ideas.

Networks are generally loose confederations of providers and can suffer from a lack of a focal point. Often networks become highly dependent on a key person to bring people together and if circumstances change, the network dissolves. Therefore in order to establish and sustain a practitioner network, people need to commit to:

■ open and honest discourse

■ sharing responsibility for organising events and meetings

■ agreeing the membership of the network

■ consensus on the broader dissemination of ideas and innovations

■ sustaining the group.

Through these principles networks can thrive, providing support for colleagues and developing practice for individuals and their families. Considering the amount of time and effort practitioners may dedicate to these networks it is important that they are given the best opportunity to survive from their inception. A strong network is an invaluable resource for all participants.

Table 6.1 Foundation Training Plan

Session	Length	Focus	Methods	Outcomes
1	1 hr	The Triad of Impairments	• Describe model of triad • Explain each component • Discuss impact of triad	Group can identify each component of the triad noting its impact
2	1 hr	Theory of Mind	• Present model of Theory of Mind • Relate to Joint Attention • Discuss effect of deficit in ToM	Group can identify difficulties arising from impaired Theory of Mind
3	1 hr	Central Coherence Theory	• Describe central coherence theory • Explain how deficit affects people • Discuss specific examples of effect	Group can relate central coherence impairment to individuals they know
4	1 hr	Executive Function	• Present idea of executive function • Note way it operates in people • Relate to effect of environment	Group can audit effect of environmental stimuli on individuals
5	1 hr	Sensory Issues	• Explain different perceptual profile • Note effect of hypo/hyper-sensitivity • Discuss implications for individuals	Group can offer strategies to moderate the effect of sensory problems

Positive Behaviour Strategies to Support Children and Young People with Autism,
Paul Chapman Publishing © Martin Hanbury, 2007

Table 6.1 (Continued)

Session	Length	Focus	Methods	Outcomes
6	1 hr	**Challenging Behaviour**	• Present definition • Explain five categories of challenge • Relate individuals to the model	Group can recognise features of challenging behaviour in individuals
7	1 hr	**Functional Analysis**	• Emphasise behaviour is needs driven • Examine four categories of need • Relate needs to individuals' behaviour	Group can relate individuals' behaviour to area of need
8	1 hr	**Proactive Strategies**	• Explain proactive strategies • Present arousal graph • Discuss optimum times for learning	Group can identify optimum learning conditions for individuals
9	1 hr	**Plenary**	• Revise learning • Address concerns and questions • Confirm and consolidate	Group can operate more effectively in supporting individuals

Positive Behaviour Strategies to Support Children and Young People with Autism,
Paul Chapman Publishing © Martin Hanbury, 2007

Key points

- Progress in the field of autism and challenging behaviour can be achieved through collaboration and mutual support.

- Changing social circumstances determine that there is a need for a broader dissemination of knowledge and understanding related to autism and challenging behaviour.

- Families are an invaluable resource for both other families and practitioners.

- Practitioners can provide overviews of developments within the field of autism and challenging behaviour for families.

- Practitioner support for other practitioners exists across three levels – namely:

  (a) Dialogue

  (b) Cascade

  (c) Network.

- Practitioners providing training should audit the knowledge and understanding of the groups they are engaged with.

- Networks of practitioners provide the opportunity for supportive and innovative practice.

APPENDIX TO CHAPTER 6

Training Materials

The following training materials are intended to provide people supporting individuals with autism and challenging behaviour with a number of options for developing practice within their organisations.

The content of the programme is arranged as eight discrete sessions which cover each of the major themes explored in this book and is intended to offer an overview of autism and the basic principles governing our understanding of behaviour support. While the structure presented relates closely to the schedule proposed in Table 6.1, people using these materials must use their own discretion in deciding how best to meets the needs of the context they are operating in.

People leading training may photocopy the following pages to offer handouts to others, use the content to produce slides on acetates or copy the content into PowerPoint presentations. The content may be supplemented with other ideas and suggestions drawn from this book or any other source in order to meet specific requirements in particular places.

Critically, people leading training need to carefully consider the pace with which they address the concepts presented among these training materials and ensure as far as is possible that a sound awareness and understanding of key issues has been reached.

Session 1

The Triad of Impairments

... we found that all children with 'autistic features', whether they fitted Kanner's or Asperger's descriptions or had bits and pieces of both, had in common absence or impairments of social interaction, communication and development of imagination. They also had a narrow, rigid, repetitive pattern of activities and interests. The three impairments (referred to as the 'triad') were shown in a wide variety of ways, but the underlying similarities were recognizable.

(Wing and Gould, 1979)

The Triad of Impairments

Impairment in **Social Communication**

Impairment in **Social Understanding**

Impairment in **Imagination**

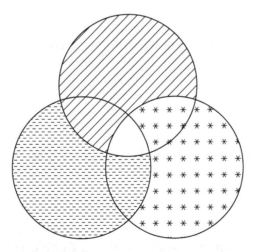

Positive Behaviour Strategies to Support Children and Young People with Autism,
Paul Chapman Publishing © Martin Hanbury, 2007

Session 2

Theory of Mind

- Theory of Mind is the ability to appreciate the **mental states** of oneself and other people.

- It enables us to understand that other people have thoughts and feelings which differ from our own.

- It is a prerequisite to effective functioning in social groups.

- It is usually evident in children from around the age of four onwards.

- Theory of Mind is indicated by young children sharing **joint attention** with other people.

- People with autism seem to lack the ability to 'think about thoughts' (Happe, 1994).

- This has been described as **mindblindness** (Baron-Cohen, 1995).

Positive Behaviour Strategies to Support Children and Young People with Autism,
Paul Chapman Publishing © Martin Hanbury, 2007

Session 3

Central Coherence Theory

■ Central Coherence Theory (Frith, 1989) describes the natural predisposition people have to place information into a **context** in order to give it meaning.

■ This gives us 'the gist' and enables us to see 'the bigger picture'.

■ People with autism tend to focus on the detail rather than the whole.

■ The failure to appreciate the whole accounts for the piecemeal way in which people with autism acquire knowledge and the unusual cognitive profile presented by many people with autism.

■ The lack of central coherence may be detected in:

1. *The narrowed interests of people with autism.*

2. *The ways in which people with autism are often unable to generalise skills.*

3. *The way in which people with autism often display areas of relative strength described as 'islets of ability'.*

Positive Behaviour Strategies to Support Children and Young People with Autism,
Paul Chapman Publishing © Martin Hanbury, 2007

Session 4

Executive Function

- Executive Function (Norman and Shallice, 1980) is the mechanism which enables us to move our attention from one activity or object to another flexibly and easily.

- It allows us to plan strategically, solve problems and set ourselves objectives.

- The absence of such a mechanism determines that:

  1. *All our actions are controlled by the environment in response to cues and stimuli, leading to apparently meaningless activity.*

  2. *Actions and behaviours compete for dominance in a disorganised and inconsistent manner, leading to an inability to plan and execute goal-generated behaviour.*

- This emerges as:

  1. *Highly distractible behaviour.*

  2. *Dependence upon ritual and routines.*

  3. *An apparent inability to plan strategically.*

Positive Behaviour Strategies to Support Children and Young People with Autism,
Paul Chapman Publishing © Martin Hanbury, 2007

Session 5

Sensory Issues

- People with autism are understood to experience significant differences in their sensory perception of the world around them (Bogdashina, 2003).

- These difficulties can result in hypo- or hyper-sensitivity in each of the following areas:

    1. *Visual*

    2. *Olfactory (smell)*

    3. *Auditory (hearing)*

    4. *Taste*

    5. *Touch.*

- This can result in extreme intolerance of some sensory stimuli.

- Alternatively, some sensory stimuli can cause extreme over-excitement.

Positive Behaviour Strategies to Support Children and Young People with Autism,
Paul Chapman Publishing © Martin Hanbury, 2007

Session 6

Challenging Behaviour

A Working Definition

Episodes or patterns of behaviour which present significant risk of harm or restriction to an individual and the people around them and are likely to be severely detrimental to the quality of life experienced by those individuals and the people around them.

- Can be categorised as:

    1. *Violence*

    2. *Self-injury*

    3. *Destruction*

    4. *Disruption*

    5. *Excessive self-stimulation.*

- 20% of children and 15% of adults with learning disabilities exhibit challenging behaviour.

- 50% of these people experience some form of physical intervention during their lifetime.

- Has associations with autism due to the nature of the difficulties people with autism encounter in meeting their fundamental needs.

Positive Behaviour Strategies to Support Children and Young People with Autism,
Paul Chapman Publishing © Martin Hanbury, 2007

Session 7

Functional Analysis

Human behaviour never occurs in a vacuum.

(LaVigna and Donnellan, 1986)

■ Human behaviour is a **function** of the context within which it occurs.

■ Behaviour is driven by an individual's **needs**.

■ Needs can be identified according to four broad categories:

  1. Attention

  2. Tangible

  3. Escape

  4. Sensory.

■ Behaviour can be **multi-functional** – it can serve several needs simultaneously.

■ Equally, several patterns of behaviour may be focused around a single area of need.

■ Understanding the function of a behaviour is prerequisite to effective **behaviour support**.

Session 8

Proactive Strategies

Proactive Strategies:

- support **positive behaviour**

- teach alternative skills to address individuals' needs

- need to occur when **arousal levels** are compatible with effective learning

- can be engaged when there are **optimum learning conditions.**

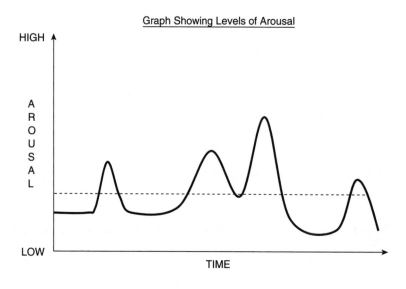

Graph Showing Levels of Arousal

Positive Behaviour Strategies to Support Children and Young People with Autism,
Paul Chapman Publishing © Martin Hanbury, 2007

GLOSSARY

behaviour management: an approach to challenging behaviour which is suggestive of one person controlling another person's behaviour through a series of externally imposed factors.

behaviour support: an approach to challenging behaviour which enables individuals to develop behaviour patterns which are productive and fulfilling for that individual.

central coherence: the natural predisposition people have to place information into a context in order to give it meaning.

executive function: the mechanism which enables us to move our attention from one activity or object to another flexibly and easily.

flexibility of thought: the capacity to think in ways which enable us to solve problems and alter our perspectives according to information we receive.

functional analysis: an effort to understand behaviour as a function of the context in which it occurs through an examination of the dynamic interplay of environment, interpersonal relationships and individuals' needs.

improved lifestyle options: an approach which enhances an individual's experience of life.

incident-specific strategies: approaches towards challenging behaviour which address present and immediate concerns.

inclusion: the notion of involving all people regardless of their difference in all aspects of society.

longitudinal data: information which is gathered over a prolonged period of time.

low arousal: an approach which consciously reduces the amount of stimuli a person experiences.

medical intervention: any intervention designed by healthcare professionals.

mindblindness: a term used to describe the condition which emanates from the inability of people with autism to appreciate other people's mental states.

Motivation Assessment Scale: a schedule of sixteen items which examine the conditions under which identified behaviour occurs, thereby providing an insight into the needs which are driving the behaviour.

optimum learning conditions: the condition under which an individual is most likely to learn effectively and enduringly.

person-centred planning: an approach towards providing holistic support for individuals with disability.

physical environment: the fabric, furnishings and fittings of an environment.

prevalence of autism: the overall number of people with autism within the population.

proactive strategies: positive and ethically sound interventions which are designed to pre-empt the occurrence of challenging behaviour.

rewards: items, objects or activities which an individual finds motivating and attractive.

social communication: the broad variety of ways in which people exchange ideas and information.

social environment: the people and relationships which exist around an individual.

social understanding: the ability to appreciate the subtle and complex social rules by which society is governed.

theory of mind: the capacity to appreciate that other people have mental states which differ from our own.

token systems: any number of items which can be collected in order to earn a reward.

triad of impairments: a conceptual model which presents autism as a condition in which individuals experience marked disability in three key domains.

Further Reading

Baron-Cohen, S. (1995) *Mindblindness:An Essay on Autism and Theory of Mind*, Bradford Books, London.

Bogdashina, O. (2003) *Sensory Perceptual Issues in Autism and Asperger Syndrome: Different Sensory Experiences – Different Perceptual Worlds*, Jessica Kingsley Publishers, London.

Durand, V. M. and Crimmins, D. B. (1992) *The Motivation Assessment Scale Administration Guide*, Monaco Associates, Topeka, KS.

Emerson, E. (2001) *Challenging Behaviour: Analysis and Intervention in People with Severe Intellectual Disabilities*, Cambridge University Press, Cambridge.

Frith, U. (1989) *Autism: Explaining the Enigma*, Basil Blackwell, Oxford.

Happe, F. (1994) *Autism: An Introduction to Psychological Theory*, UCL Press, London.

Jordan, R. and Powell, S. (1995) *Understanding and Teaching Children with Autism*, John Wiley, Chichester.

LaVigna, G. W. and Donnellan, A. M. (1986) *Alternatives to Punishment: Solving Problems with Non-aversive Strategies*, Irvington Publishers, New York.

Norman, D. and Shallice, T. (1980) 'Attention to action: willed and automatic control of behaviour', In *Consciousness and Self-regulation*, Vol. 4 (ed. Davidson, R., Schwartz, G. and Shapiro, D.), Plenum Press, New York.

United Nations (1948) *Universal Declaration of Human Rights*, UNESCO, Paris.

Whitaker, P. (2001) *Challenging Behaviour and Autism*, The National Autistic Society, London.

Wing, L. (1996) *The Autistic Spectrum*, Constable and Robinson, London.

Wing, L. and Gould, J. (1979) 'Severe impairments of social interaction and associated abnormalities in children: epidemiology and classification', *Journal of Autism and Childhood Schizophrenia*, 9, 11–29.

INDEX

Added to a page number 'f' denotes a figure and 't' denotes a table

Franklin Pierce College Library

00171052